RAF DUXFORD

Michael Evans

Essex County Council

First Published 2012
Copyright © Michael Evans 2012
Michael Evans asserts his moral rights to
be identified as the author of this work.

Bretwalda Books
Unit 8, Fir Tree Close, Epsom,
Surrey KT17 3LD

info@BretwaldaBooks.com

To receive an e-catalogue of our complete
range of books send an email to
info@BretwaldaBooks.com

ISBN 978-1-907791-74-1

Bretwalda Books Ltd

CHAPTER ONE:
Introduction 4

CHAPTER TWO:
The Early Years 6

CHAPTER THREE:
Off to War 21

CHAPTER FOUR:
The Battle of Britain Begins 36

CHAPTER FIVE:
The Duxford Wing 50

CHAPTER SIX:
All Change at Duxford 71

CHAPTER SEVEN:
The American Intervention 87

CHAPTER EIGHT:
D-Day and Beyond 100

CHAPTER NINE:
The Cold War 112

CHAPTER TEN:
Epilogue: The Station that Refused to Die 123

Index 128

Introduction

The history of RAF Duxford dates back nearly 95 years and apart from a very few short breaks, this legendary airfield has been active for all of that time.

The airfield's origins lie in the second half of the Great War. By 1917, more training establishments were needed for the fledgling flying arm of the army – and an early choice for a training airfield was an area close to the village of Duxford, eight miles south of Cambridge. By the time that building work was completed, the war had actually ended, but this had not stopped the new airfield from being used to train aircrew and ground crews, many of whom came direct from the United States.

Once the war ended, Duxford continued as a flying training school. However, come 1923, it became a fighter base and would continue in this role until 1961.

With such a long life there have inevitably been a number of iconic highlights. In 1935 it hosted King George V's Silver Jubilee Flypast, with 182 aircraft in a formation that stretched for nine miles across the Cambridgeshire countryside. In 1938 it was the station where No.19 Squadron received the first Supermarine Spitfire to enter RAF service.

Many famous squadrons have been associated with Duxford over the years and among the countless numbers of personnel are many who can be included in the ranks of "true heroes".

Keith Park, who later became commander of 11 Group, responsible for the defence of London during the Battle of Britain, was a squadron commander at Duxford in the 1920s. It was during the Battle of Britain that the Duxford squadrons developed the controversial 'Big Wing' that was regarded with such disapproval by Keith Park, but was so favoured by Trafford Leigh-Mallory, commander of Number 12 Group and Douglas Bader, CO of No.242 Squadron.

Following the Battle of Britain Duxford became the home of a number of specialised units, including the Air Fighting Development Unit with its

KEITH PARK
New Zealander Keith Park served in the Royal Flying Corps during WW I. In 1927 he became commander of 111 Squadron at Duxford and later controller of No 11 Group during the Battle of Britain.

collection of captured German aircraft that were used for evaluation purposes after they had been restored to flying condition.

For 30 months from March 1943 to the ending of hostilities, Duxford was the home to the three squadrons of the USAAF 78th Fighter Group. During that period the American airmen flew 450 missions, destroyed 697 enemy aircraft and lost 180 pilots. The Group received two Distinguished Unit Citations. Following its return to the RAF, for 16 years Duxford was heavily involved in the protection of Britain during the Cold War, but priorities change and 43 years of service life came to an end in 1961 when the RAF moved out.

Apart from a burst of action in 1968 when the airfield was used during the making of the star-studded film *Battle of Britain*, things were very quiet until in 1971 when the Imperial War Museum began to take an interest. It had been looking for somewhere to store, restore and possibly display some of its larger exhibits.

One thing led to another and the last three decades have seen this historic airfield become the home of a unique and internationally acclaimed museum where history really is in the air. Regular air displays of vintage aircraft throughout the summer months continue to ensure that after more than 90 years Duxford continues to be a living airfield.

The Early Years

As the bells rang out for the beginning of the twentieth century, in the eyes of most Europeans the world had never seemed more prosperous and stable. The empires of Europe controlled and encircled the globe and trade and prosperity continued to grow.

While it was true that there were already worrying signs of a rise in international tensions, there had been no major European war since 1815. Very few of the New Year revellers would have thought that within 14 years the military might that had allowed Europe to dominate the world would suddenly be turned on itself. Still less would they have accepted that this would lead to a terrifying demonstration of the destructive power of industrially produced weapons.

This was a period of advancing technology and in July 1909 Louis Blériot won the London Daily Mail's £1,000 prize for being the first person to cross the English Channel in a heavier than air craft. Astute tacticians soon realised

ROYAL FLYING CORPS POSTER
This Royal Flying Corps recruiting poster dates from 1913. Men were required for various trades for pay ranging from 2/- (10p) to 9/- (45p) per day. Pilots could receive as much as 13/- a day (65p).

LIEUTENANT-GENERAL JAN SMUTS
The War Office and the Navy both wanted control of British air power and Lloyd George gave Lieutenant-General Smuts the task of conducting a review. Following his recommendation an independent RAF came into being on 1st April 1918.

the military potential of aircraft and on 13th April 1912, King George V signed the royal warrant establishing the Royal Flying Corps (usually abbreviated to RFC) and by the end of the year there were 133 officers with 12 manned balloons and 36 aircraft.

When the war with Germany began on 4th August 1914, Britain had around 113 aircraft in military service. Of these the RFC sent four squadrons to France; numbers 2, 3, 4 and 5. Each squadron had 12 aircraft and with other aircraft in depots this gave a total strength in France of 63 aircraft, supported by 900 men.

Very early on it became clear that the Royal Flying Corps was going to make a valuable contribution. Up until that time cavalry units had carried out most reconnaissance duties, but because of the trench deadlock this was no longer possible. The use of aircraft was the obvious answer. It was not for another year or so that the possibilities of dropping bombs and mounting machine guns in aircraft began to be exploited.

Before long, the rapid expansion of the Royal Flying Corps and the Royal Naval Air Service was leading to a whole range of organisational problems and some form of streamlining was necessary. The War Office and the Admiralty both felt that their influence should be paramount in air matters, but the Prime Minister, David Lloyd George decided to ask the eminent South African, Lieutenant-General Jan Smuts to look at the matter as an impartial observer and to report back.

THE DUKE OF YORK, TRENCHARD AND COURTNEY
The 24-year-old Duke of York, later King George VI, with Major-General Sir Hugh Trenchard and Colonel C L Courtney at the Independent Air Force Dinner held on 14th July 1919 at the Savoy Hotel, London.

In his report of August 1917 General Smuts recommended that a completely independent service should be set up with an Air Minister and an air staff. The War Cabinet approved the recommendation, and on 1 April 1918 the RAF came into being. This was the first independent air force in the world and Major-General Sir Hugh Trenchard was appointed the first Chief of Air Staff.

The massive expansion of the RFC obviously put a considerable strain on recruiting, training and aircraft supply. As part of the need for more Training Depot Stations, two Cambridgeshire villages, Duxford and neighbouring

Fowlmere, were selected as sites for fully-fledged aerodromes. Situated only three miles from each other, their close proximity ensured that their development and future history were inevitably intertwined.

The site of Duxford airfield was 223 acres of farmland to the south of the Newmarket to Royston Road (now the A505), with a further 15 acres on the other side of the road.

Construction contracts for both airfields were let to P & W Anderson Ltd of Aberdeen and work began in October 1917. The estimated cost of Duxford airfield was put at £90,000. Duxford opened on 1st March 1918 when No.19 and No.129 Squadrons were formed as day bomber squadrons, but in the end neither ever became operational.

In addition to pilots, the expansion programme had also brought an urgent need for more ground crews. The US Government had agreed that up to 15,000 newly recruited air mechanics should serve at the British flying schools. The first American mechanics arrived on 15 March for a five-month training stint. By July the airfield was under the control of the new RAF and that month No.35 Training Depot Station finally opened at Duxford having moved from Thetford and coming under the control of No.26 Wing in Cambridge. At the same time No.31 Training Depot Station opened at Fowlmere.

On 1st September 1918, No.123 Squadron RFC arrived from Waddington and shortly afterwards three more American aero engineer squadrons arrived. Their work was primarily running motor transport and assembling the aircraft. Like the personnel, everything arrived at nearby Whittlesford railway station, with all the aircraft in packing cases.

The official opening of RAF Duxford came in September 1918, even though work on finishing the airport was still not complete. The final cost was put at £460,000 resulting in War Ministry holding an enquiry to see why the cost of construction was more than five times the original estimate.

Although the training programme progressed, the fortunes of the War had changed. The German land forces were now in retreat and by October when the men of 159 US Aero Squadron were finally ready to leave for France, Germany was already suing for peace. By now 123 Squadron had been disbanded.

The war ended on 11th November and two days later the order came from the US military to close down all US aviation activity in the British Isles. Within days the Americans had left Duxford.

At this point the RAF training depot's staff numbered 450 men and 158 women. The women were members of the Women's Royal Air Force that had been founded in May 1918. Initially formed to train women as mechanics, thereby freeing men for more active roles, but as time went on members of the WRAF undertook many other roles that had previously been the preserve of their male counterparts.

By the end of November the chief concern of both Duxford and Fowlmere was the disbandment and demobilisation of squadrons returning from the continent. Although building work on both airfields was now more or less complete, the need for airfields had diminished. The new RAF still had a training commitment, but there was no longer a need for two Training Depots in such close proximity.

It was decided that Duxford, with its better road and rail links would be kept going as a permanent RAF flying training station, but that Fowlmere would close.

The future of RAF Duxford seemed assured, but there were still some doubts as to what that future might hold.

By the end of the war the RAF had 22,000 aircraft in 188 operational squadrons with 293,532 officers and men, but within two years this had been reduced to 371 aircraft in 12 squadrons with 31,500 officers and men. It was not only the numbers of aircraft and men that was reduced, the WRAF was disbanded in 1920. Things might have gone further, but Lord Trenchard, the so-called 'father of the Royal Air Force', was determined to prevent the army and the navy from contriving to disband the RAF and to re-form their own air arms using former RAF aircraft and aircrews.

So Trenchard cleverly structured his tiny RAF using a series of fairly modest units that would be capable of later expansion should the need arise. These included the RAF College at Cranwell for the training of officers, the School of Technical Training at Halton for boy entrants or apprentices, the Central Flying School for training Instructors and Training Schools for pilots.

It was decided that the newly completed RAF Duxford would be an important element in the RAF's training commitment, while nearby the equally new RAF Fowlmere was to close. However, in the short term at least, both stations were more concerned with disbandment and demobilisation as planes and men flew in from France.

For a while Fowlmere was used to store the giant Handley Page 0/400 bombers, but the airfield was finally abandoned in 1922. The following year all the buildings and hard standings were demolished without trace and the whole site reverted to farmland.

Meanwhile it was all activity at Duxford. In 1919 Number 8 Squadron arrived with its Bristol F.2Bs (Bristol Fighters), to be disbanded the following year. By June 1920 the station took up its designated role as a training station. Initially there were 27 officers, 390 other ranks and 12 pupils. For the next three years Number 2 Flying Training School used the airfield with eighteen Avro 504, eighteen Bristol F.2B and four DH9A aircraft.

All three types were biplanes. The Avro 504 had been in service since 1913 and almost 9,000 were built. It was an Avro 504 that had the dubious distinction of being the first British aircraft to be shot down in the war. It quickly became obsolete as a frontline aircraft, but it came into its own as a trainer. Following the end of the war it became the standard trainer of the RAF. More than 300 surplus 504s were placed on the civilian register in Britain and they continued flying in large numbers until well into the 1930s.

The Bristol F.2B Bristol Fighters were introduced in the middle of the war and well over 5,000 were manufactured before production finally stopped in the late 1920s. It was a two-seater fighter, but was surprisingly agile and well able to hold its own against enemy single-seaters.

TRENCHARD
In 1918, he briefly served as the first Chief of the Air Staff before taking up command of the Independent Air Force in France. He spent the next ten years securing the future of the RAF.

The DH.9A was a light bomber and flew for the first time in April 1918, just seven months before the end of the war. 2,250 had been ordered and the first ones were delivered in June, with 885 completed by the end of the year. It was decided that the DH.9A would be a standard type in the new RAF and the majority of the outstanding orders were fulfilled. In the years between 1920 and 1931, 24 squadrons, at home and abroad, were equipped with DH.9A aircraft.

THE ARMSTRONG-WHITWORTH SISKIN
The Siskin was one of the first new RAF fighters to enter service after World War I. It was noted for its aerobatic qualities and presented thrilling exhibitions of flying at every RAF display from 1925 to 1931.

Number 2 Flying Training School improved rapidly to the point that other activities could be undertaken. These activities included early experiments in aerial photography and mapping, with aircraft flying all over East Anglia. At the 1921 Hendon Air Pageant there was a competition to see who was best at this new form of technology and the team from RAF Duxford managed to beat the RAF School of Photography into second place.

In April 1923 the Steel-Bartholomew Committee for the Defence of Southeast England established an Air Fighting Zone bordered by a line stretching from Duxford to Devises. This led to a limited expansion of the RAF and a training flight of Sopwith Snipes was added to the School. On 1st April 1923 pilots and aircraft at Duxford re-formed two new fighter squadrons; numbers No.19 and No.29. Both had seen distinguished service on the Western Front, but both had been disbanded on 31st December 1919.

As is always the case, squadrons came and went, but for the next 18 years No.19 Squadron was to become part of the life of RAF Duxford. No.19 and No.29 Squadrons were joined by No.111 Squadron after it was reformed on 1st October 1923. Initially No.19 Squadron was somewhat under No.111's shadow, but both squadrons came to take on something of an iconic status, particularly in the area of aerobatics.

In June 1924, under new Home Defence arrangements, it was decided that Number 2 Flying Training School should be moved to RAF Digby in Lincolnshire and Duxford would officially become a fighter station – and it remained so for the next 37 years.

Also in June 1924, No.111 Squadron added a third flight of Armstrong Whitworth Siskin IIIs and began trials in high altitude air combat. This task continued for a while, with various changes and improvements being made to the aircraft. It was during this time that No.111 Squadron began to build up its reputation for close formation flying and aerobatics. In January 1925 its Grebes and Snipes were retired and the squadron became fully equipped with Siskins, which they were to keep until January 1931.

January 1925 also brought the formation of the Meteorological Flight at Duxford. Initially there were just two aircraft, but as time went on the Flight used a variety of aircraft including Siskins, Hawker Woodcocks, Bristol Bulldogs, Westland Wallaces and Gloster Grebes. This was often highly dangerous work, with aircraft taking off in conditions that would normally be regarded as quite unsuitable for flying. Duxford was to be its base for eleven years until it moved to Mildenhall in late 1936.

The Cambridge University Air Squadron formed at Duxford on 1 October 1925, starting a link that was to continue until the beginning of World War II. In May 1918, a wealthy benefactor called Emile Mond had endowed a Chair of Aeronautical Engineering at the University in memory of his son Francis, who had been killed while flying in France. The endowment had been on condition that the RAF made available facilities nearby for research in flight.

The RAF had encouraged this relationship, hoping that interested undergraduates might wish to join the service as officers. Flying training began in February 1926 using Avro 504s. By 1933 the 504s had been replaced by Avro Tutors and the squadron remained at Duxford until the outbreak of World War II when it moved to Marshall's new aerodrome on Newmarket Road in Cambridge.

A noted member of the University Air Squadron was Ft/Lt Frank Whittle, who was studying engineering at the university and regularly flew at Duxford. It was Frank Whittle, later to become Air Commodore Sir Frank Whittle, who first thought about using a jet turbine as a means of powering an aircraft. This eventually lead to the production of the first British jet-powered fighter, the Gloster Meteor, in 1943.

In 1927 a new commander arrived for No.111 Squadron. He was Sqn Ldr Keith Park who was later to become commander of 11 Group responsible for the defence of London and Southeast England during the Battle of Britain.

By 1927, at the age of 35, Park had already had an eventful life. He was born in New Zealand, the son of a Scottish geologist and after some time in the merchant navy he joined the New Zealand Field Artillery as a Territorial. He took part in the Gallipoli landings of April 1915 as an NCO, but three months later was commissioned as a second lieutenant. After a number of months of squalor in the trenches he decided to transfer from the New Zealand Army to the British Army and he joined the Royal Horse and Field Artillery.

In January 1916 he was evacuated from Gallipoli and shipped to France where he took part in the Battle of the Somme. In October 1916 a German shell blew him off his horse and he was later certified as being 'unfit for service' in the horse artillery, by which was meant that he could no longer ride a horse. In December 1916 he joined the Royal Flying Corps.

He was posted to No.48 Squadron flying Bristol Fighters and in due course became squadron commander. He achieved much, both as a pilot and

AVRO TUTOR

The Avro Tutor was a two-seat biplane from the interwar period. It was a simple but rugged initial trainer that was used by the RAF as well as many other air forces worldwide.

---

as a commander. He was awarded a Military Cross and Bar, a Distinguished Flying Cross and the French Croix de Guerre. After the war he was awarded a permanent commission in the new Royal Air Force.

★★★

March 1928 saw the beginning of a major four-year expansion of RAF Duxford By this date No.19 Squadron was the only resident squadron, taking over No.111's mantle as aerobatic squadron, initially using Armstrong Whitworth Siskin III aircraft, but re-equipping with Bristol Bulldog IIAs in 1931.

During the early 1930s Bulldog IIAs became the most widely used aircraft in the RAF. 268 were built and they had a maximum speed of just under 180 mph with a range of 300 miles. The Bulldog's popularity in the RAF stems

HARRY BROADHURST
Harry Broadhurst, commonly known as Broady, developed his skills as an aerobatic pilot while at Duxford. He went on to become Station Commander at RAF Wittering and was acknowleged as being one of the great wartime leaders.

from its cheap maintenance, and its ability to trail smoke during formation aerobatics.

At the beginning of 1935 No.19 Squadron became the first to fly the RAF's fastest new fighter, the Gloster Gauntlet. This fighter was capable of 230 mph and the display team led by Flight Lieutenant, later Wing Cdr, Harry Broadhurst became famous for their daring three-aircraft formations with their wings tied together.

As a young man Harry Broadhurst's plan to join the RAF had been thwarted by his father, a retired army officer, who had insisted that he joined the Territorial Army. Since Broadhurst Junior was under age, he had no option but to do what his father wanted and he was commissioned as a Second Lieutenant in the Royal Artillery in May 1925. In October the following year, whilst still under age, he persuaded his CO to sign his application for secondment to the RAF. His father's reaction to this is not recorded.

Broadhurst soon qualified as a pilot and joined No.11 Squadron at Netheravon. In February 1928 he was appointed to a Short Service Commission in the RAF and he resigned from the army. At the end of 1928, No.11 Squadron moved to India and Broadhurst was later 'Mentioned in Dispatches' while serving on the North West Frontier.

Three years later he returned to the UK and joined No.41 Squadron flying Bristol Bulldogs at Northolt and in October he was received a Medium Service Commission. During his time with No.41 Squadron his reputation began to grow due to the excellent team and solo aerobatic displays that he performed at the Hendon Air Pageants. He was also recognised as a fine marksman and for three years in a row he won the Sassoon Trophy for air-to-air firing.

He arrived in Duxford in November 1933 when he became Flight Commander of No.19 Squadron. He built on his reputation as a great leader, leading the squadron's display team of five Bulldogs

The Silver Jubilee Year of King George V came in 1935 and on 6th July the King came to Duxford and took the salute at a Fly Past of 20 RAF squadrons. In all, 182 aircraft took part in a formation that stretched for nine miles in length. No.19 Squadron gave a special display of aerobatics.

In addition to King George and Queen Mary, distinguished guests included the Prince of Wales, later King Edward VIII, the Duke of York who was later to become King George VI and Lord Trenchard, Marshal of the Royal Air Force. More than 100,000 members of the public came to see the spectacle. Special guests had lunch in what is now Duxford's Number 5 Hanger.

In 1936, after No.19 squadron re-equipped with the new Gloster Gauntlets, Broadhurst continued to lead the aerobatic display team and in June he was awarded a permanent commission at the rank of Flight Lieutenant. Leaving the squadorn at the end of the year after being posted to RAF Abu Sueir in Egypt as an Instructor. Broadhurst went on to become Station Commander of RAF Wittering and was acknowledged as being one of the great wartime leaders.

★★★

In July 1936 No.66 Squadron was formed at Duxford from officers and ground staff of No.19 Squadron's C Flight. Equipped with Gloster Gauntlets, this new squadron joined No.19 Squadron in perfecting combat techniques with these new and up-to-date aircraft.

Although there remained a strong body of opinion that the Great War had been the 'war to end all wars', there was an equally strong body that saw war clouds were already beginning to loom. They urged the need for preparation in case the first group were being over optimistic.

A prominent member of this second group was the Commanding Officer of RAF Fighter Command, Air Chief Marshal Sir Hugh Dowding. Dowding could be described as a dour Scot and was universally known as 'Stuffy Dowding'. Fighter Command came into being on 1st May 1936 under Dowding, tasked with defending Britain from air attack. At first Number 11 Group with its headquarters in Uxbridge assumed operational and administrative control of the southern section, while Number 12 Group controlled the northern section from its headquarters at Watnall in Nottinghamshire.

Subsequently four other groups were added; Number 13 Group for the area north of York; Number 10 Group for the area west of Oxford; Number 14 Group for the area north of the Tay and Number 9 Group for South West England. RAF Duxford was initially placed in Number 11 Group but it was subsequently transferred to Number 12 Group, becoming the southernmost station in that Group.

Crucial elements in Dowding's strategy included radar, human observers, efficient plotting of incoming raids and radio control of the advanced fighter aircraft that would be sent up to intercept the raiders.

These advanced fighting aircraft included the renowned Spitfires and Hurricanes that were later to feature so prominently at Duxford. On 4 August 1938 No.19 Squadron received its first Spitfire when Jeffrey Quill, Supermarine's chief test pilot flew into Duxford in Spitfire K9789. This was actually the third production Spitfire and Quill had taken it up for its final factory test and decided that since all was well he would deliver it in person.

There were several reasons for choosing No.19 as the first Spitfire squadron. One of course was the squadron's reputation, but another important factor was that its CO, Sqn/Ldr Henry Cozens had a degree in aeronautical engineering. Duxford had also recently been enlarged making it capable of coping with the faster Spitfires. Finally the squadron was based within easy reach of London and the various VIPs who would want to monitor the entry of the Spitfire into operational service.

After delivery, it was a week before K9789 flew again. During that time it was completely stripped down and examined by the station engineers, but on 11th August Sq/Ldr Cozens got his chance to fly the new plane. He later recalled that, "It was like flying a lorry at low levels and low speeds, but once you had reached 10,000 feet the true characteristics became apparent and it was delightful to fly".

Station Commander, Wg/Cdr Lester bagged the next flight. 11th August was the day that No.19 Squadron got its second Spitfire, K9790, with the third, K9792 arriving on 16 August. A pattern was then established of new Spitfires arriving at the rate of about one a week. The Spitfires of No.66 Squadron's were slower to arrive. Its first machine, K9802 was formally

GLOSTER GAUNTLET
The Gloster Gauntlet was a single-seat, biplane fighter designed and built by Gloster Aircraft in the 1930s. It was the last RAF fighter to have an open cockpit and the RAF's penultimate biplane fighter.

handed over just before the end of October 1938 and No.66 promptly joined in the process of evaluation and familiarisation. By the end of the year both squadrons were up to strength making them operational on Spitfires. Trials of improvements and new equipment continued well into the New Year.

Accidents were inevitable in those early days. The doubtful honour of being the first pilot to crash a Spitfire went to 22-year-old P/O Gordon Sinclair from No.19 Squadron. He was landing after his first flight in aircraft K9792 on 3rd November when the port undercarriage leg collapsed under him and the aircraft flipped over onto its back. The accident was not Sinclair's fault, but the aircraft was a write-off.

Sinclair was incredibly lucky to escape with barely a scratch – and this luck was to stay with him throughout the war. Although having to bail out at least twice, he scored ten victories and he eventually retired as a Wing Commander in 1957.

On 24th May 1939 the country celebrated Empire Day and as had been the usual practice since 1934, Duxford and other RAF stations were open to the public. This year, with its politically uncertain future, all previous records were broken and 12,000 people attended the display at Duxford. In 1939 these displays were an important part of the RAF recruitment campaign and enthralled crowds watched displays dominated by the new Hurricanes, Spitfires, Wellingtons and Blenheims.

In August No.611 Squadron, another Spitfire squadron went to Duxford for its Summer Camp and was still there when war was declared at 11.00 am on Sunday 3rd September 1939. This meant that at the outbreak of war, of the RAF's nine operational Spitfire squadrons, three were at Duxford.

Off to War

B y the outbreak of war on 3rd September 1939, 306 Spitfires had been delivered to squadrons, but 36 of these had already been written off in training accidents.

Writing off a Spitfire was an expensive business. In 1939 a Spitfire cost £9,500, which at today's prices would be around £480,000. The Rolls-Royce Merlin engine that then cost £2,000 would now be £100,000 and even the clock, which was £2:10s:0d in 1939 would today cost around £120.

SPITFIRE THUMBS UP

Spitfire pilots were usually regarded as the *crème de la crème*. Spitfires were beautiful aircraft to fly but required a fair amount of skill if accidents were to be avoided, especially when landing

BADER IN HURRICANE
In February 1940, Douglas Bader returned to the RAF where he joined 19 Squadron at Duxford flying Spitfires. Four months later he was given command of 242 Squadron flying Hurricanes.

When the war began, the RAF had nine fully equipped Spitfire squadrons. No.19, No.66 and No.611 were at Duxford while No.54, No.65 and No.74 were at Hornchurch. No.72 was at Church Fenton, No.41 and No.609 were at Catterick and No.602 was at Abbotsinch. The tenth was to be No.603 Squadron at Turnhouse, replacing its Gladiators with Spitfires.

Early in the war it was felt that if and when an invasion should come, it would most likely be along the East Coast with its gently shelving beaches, behind which there was relatively flat country where tanks could easily advance towards London or the industrial Midlands. RAF Duxford firmly expected to be in the front line.

Accidents during training were common. One of the first casualties of the war occurred at Duxford and involved a Spitfire. Three days after its outbreak, on 6th September 1939, Pilot Officer Douglas Paton of No.66 Squadron is reported to have crashed Spitfire K9986 while practicing night circuits. Pilot Officer Paton's grave is among 50 graves cared for by the Commonwealth War Graves Commission in the churchyard of the parish church of SS Mary and Andrew in the nearby village of Whittlesford. There are 28 graves from World War II.

A near miss occurred on 5th October 1939 when Acting Flight Lieutenant Wilf Clouston flying Spitfire K9854 was in collision with Spitfire K9821 that was being flown by Pilot Officer G E Bell. They were on their way back to Duxford from RAF Watton, west of Norwich. The propeller of Ball's aircraft chopped off most of the tail of Clouston's aircraft. Thankfully, neither pilot was injured, with Clouston managing to make a forced landing on Newmarket racecourse. Clouston, a New Zealander, survived the War and retired as a Wing Commander with 4 confirmed and 2 shared kills.

While more than 200 Hurricanes and their pilots flew out to France in the weeks after war began, Duxford's Spitfire squadrons spent their time joining in mainly routine coastal patrols and there was very little action. These patrols were carried out from RAF Horsham St Faiths, now Norwich International Airport. Training and evaluation flights continued, with No.66 Squadron working on experiments with VHF radio. These were very successful, but there were serious problems with respect to supply.

On 5 October another squadron joined the Duxford strength when No.222 Squadron was reformed flying Blenheim Mk.1Fs. The squadron's initial role was shipping protection. Meanwhile on 10th October No.611 Squadron moved to RAF Digby in Lincolnshire.

The winter of 1939-40 was extremely cold, with temperatures regularly dropping below zero. Duxford became snowed in and there were very few flying days in January. The boredom was relieved when, on 25th December 1939 and immediately before King George VI's first wartime Christmas message, a greeting was broadcast on the BBC from a pilot of No.66 Squadron as he flew over Duxford.

The first proper action seen by Duxford squadrons took place on 11th January 1940 while No.66 Squadron was on duty at Horsham St Faiths. A Heinkel He111 was attacking a trawler and after No.66 was scrambled, it was intercepted by three Spitfires. The Heinkel's port engine was damaged, but after the enemy aircraft disappeared in cloud and the Spitfires returned to base. The Heinkel was later reported to have reached Denmark before crashing.

At the end of January No.222 Squadron lost one of its pilots in an accident when Pilot Officer David Maynard was killed when his Blenheim, L6614, hit a hill near Royston while flying in poor visibility. He is buried in Whittlesford churchyard along with two other No.222 pilots who were killed during the following eight weeks.

A name that is always associated with Duxford is Douglas Bader, who joined No.19 Squadron at Duxford on 7 February 1940. At the age of 29 he was considerably older than most of his fellow pilots and his commanding officer was his old friend Squadron Leader Geoffrey Stephenson.

Bader had been forced to leave the RAF after losing both his lower legs in a flying accident, and was now very excited to be back into squadron life, particularly as he was able to fly the wonderful new Spitfire. It soon became apparent that in some circumstances Bader's lack of legs gave him a big advantage. A problem for many fighter pilots was that when they pulled high 'g-forces' in combat turns they often 'blacked out' as the flow of blood drained from the brain to other parts of the body, usually the legs. Since Bader had no legs he was able to remain conscious for longer.

Like a number of pilots, Bader had strong ideas about aerial combat that were not in accordance with the officially accepted view of the RAF. He believed in using the sun and altitude to ambush the enemy, while the conventional view was to attack the enemy in a tight formation, but Bader obeyed orders and his skill rapidly saw him promoted to section leader.

Between February and May, along with the other pilots in the squadron, Bader practiced formation flying and air tactics, as well as taking part in patrols over sea convoys. As with most of the Duxford sorties these were usually carried out after flying up to RAF Horsham St Faiths, which being near Norwich was closer to the North Sea. Since this airfield was still under construction, there was no accommodation, so the procedure was for three aircraft from No.19 Squadron to be sent up from Duxford each day.

Training accidents were still common. On Thursday 29th February 1940 Pilot Officer Horace Trenchard of No.19 Squadron, a 28-year-old New Zealander from Lower Hutt, Wellington was practicing night circuits and landings in Spitfire I K9809. He took off at about 8.25 pm and shortly afterwards made a sudden turn to port at 1200 feet, lost altitude, then dived into the ground 1½ miles NE of Duxford. He is also buried at Whittlesford.

On 31st March while taking off for one of the Horsham St Faith's convoy patrols even Douglas Bader managed to write off a Spitfire. Bader was always full of enthusiasm and skill, but initially had a hard time coming to grips with the Spitfire.

When the first batch of Spitfires had arrived at Duxford they had been fitted with fixed pitch two-blade propellers, resulting in the aircraft needing an inordinate length of runway in order to get into the air. This problem was overcome by fitting a variable pitch propeller, but it remained critical to set the propeller to fine pitch before take off. On this occasion that is what Bader forgot to do.

Bader was leading his section on a short run of the airfield and slightly down wind. In normal circumstances this would have carried minimal risk and would have saved a great deal of time. Half way through take off the other two pilots realised what Bader had failed to do and opening their throttles wide just managed to clear the boundary fence.

Unfortunately Bader didn't. He hit the fence, cartwheeled across a ploughed field and his Spitfire came to rest with the engine pushed back into the cockpit. The aircraft was a complete write-off, as were Bader's artificial legs.

Thankfully Bader had a spare set of legs, but they were a bit uncomfortable. One night while he was filing away at them in an attempt to trim them, he kept disturbing Sgt George Unwin, later Wing Commander Unwin. The new Walt Disney film *Snow White and the Seven Dwarfs* had just been released and when Unwin kept complaining, Bader retorted with: "Oh shut up Grumpy!" The name stuck and for the remainder of his distinguished RAF career and beyond, Unwin was forever known as 'Grumpy'.

SPITFIRE PILOTS RUNNING, 1939
Spitfires lined up ready for takeoff. The call to scramble has come, the groundcrews have started the engines and the pilots, weighed down by flying gear and parachutes, are running to their aircraft.

DUXFORD OPS ROOM

The Ops Room at Duxford set up as it would have been during the Battle of Britain. WAAF plotters would be moving coloured markers on the table to show attackers and defenders.

Bader was not with No.19 Squadron for very long before he was transferred to No.222 (Natal) Squadron flying Blenheims. This squadron was commanded by another old friend of Bader's, Squadron Leader 'Tubby' Mermagen. Each Duxford squadron was divided into two flights, A and B and Bader was put in charge of No.222's B Flight. Shortly after his transfer, No.222 Squadron began exchanging its Blenheim Mk IFs for Spitfires.

One young Pilot Officer, who was posted to Bader's Flight direct from Cranwell and flying training school was 19-year-old Tim Vigors. His first impression of Bader was that of "a broad-shouldered, dark-haired determined looking flight lieutenant with piercing blue eyes who was much older than the rest of them".

Bader told Vigors that he hated formality and insisted on being called Douglas. He also said that since he had trained on Gloster Gladiators, apart from Bader and Tubby Mermagen, he was the only member of the squadron familiar with single engined aircraft so he and Bader would have the job of collecting the squadron's new Spitfires from the Supermarine factory in Southampton.

A fairly brief conversion course at Duxford involving about four flights was followed by a week flying backwards and forwards to Southampton, in an Avro Anson on the way down and in a Spitfire on the way back. During that week between them they managed to collect nearly all of the Spitfires that were ready for them. In spite of a ten-year age gap and a difference in rank, a close friendship developed between Bader and Vigors.

On 10th May German forces invaded the Low Countries, Winston Churchill became Prime Minister and No.264 Squadron moved down to Duxford from Wittering with its Boulton Paul Defiants.

During the next two weeks, as the Germans advanced, the British Expeditionary Force was pushed ever closer to the sea. There was plenty of action and a great deal of movement of Squadrons in and out of Duxford at this time. On 16th May No.19 Squadron moved back to Duxford from Horsham St Faiths where it had been for most of the past month and No.66 Squadron moved up to Horsham St Faiths to take its place. After four years of being something of fixture at Duxford, over the next five years No.66 Squadron was to move 35 times.

By late May all seemed to be lost for the BEF, but then came Operation Dynamo, which saw a total of 338,226 allied troops rescued from the beaches of Dunkirk.

On 25th May, together with No.222 Squadron, No.19 Squadron moved to Hornchurch for ten days to support the Dunkirk evacuation and relieve the squadrons of 11 Group. No.264 was sent to Manston for the same reason. To provide cover for Duxford during this period No.92 Squadron arrived with their Spitfires

The full evacuation from Dunkirk began late on Sunday 26th May and lasted until Tuesday 4th June. During this time the Luftwaffe took every opportunity to bomb the beaches, although the sand softened many of the explosions. Bad weather also helped the Allies by keeping the German aircraft grounded for some of the time. In those nine days, the RAF flew 4,822 sorties over Dunkirk. Losses to the RAF were put at 177 aircraft with 240 losses to the Luftwaffe.

During their time at Hornchurch, No.19 Squadron met the Luftwaffe on five occasions, claiming 28 victories with nine probables. On that first Sunday Gordon Sinclair, the pilot who had written off the first Spitfire shot down a Bf109 on his first sortie and another on his second, although this was unconfirmed. The following day he shot down two bombers, although again neither was a confirmed kill. On 1st June he destroyed a Bf109 and shared in the destruction of a second before accounting for two bombers later in the day. At the end of June Sinclair was awarded the DFC. Three pilots were lost, including the squadron commander, Squadron Leader Geoffrey Stephenson who was shot down on the first day.

A major problem for the RAF was that they were using techniques for attack that had been developed in the days of open cockpits when there were no radios and when all communications had to be done by hand signals. These textbook tactics required aircraft to attack in tight formations. Keeping these formations required great concentration and provided little opportunity to keep a look out for any enemy attack.

As George Unwin later commented: "Our tight formations were all very well for the Hendon Air Pageant but useless in combat. Geoffrey Stephenson was a prime example; without modern combat experience he flew by the book – and was shot down by it."

Geoffrey Stephenson became a POW on 26th May, the day he was shot down, and while at Stalag Luft I he acted as Senior British Officer. Following a number of moves he eventually ended up at Oflag IV-C, better known as Colditz Castle. After the War he returned to the Central Flying School as Commandant before becoming ADC to King George VI and later to The Queen. He was killed in a flying accident on 8th November 1954 while testing a USAF F-100A at Eglin Air Base in Florida.

Following the loss of Sq/Ldr Stephenson, Ft Lt Brian Lane was made temporary CO of No.19 Squadron until Sq/Ldr Philip Pinkham arrived from St Athan Air Fighting School on 10th June.

Another 20-year-old Pilot Officer Peter (Watty) Watson was also lost at this time after being hit by a cannon shell fired by a Bf109. Although seen to bail out, he died and is buried in the Calais Canadian War Cemetery. Later that day the squadron flew another patrol and again they were 'bounced' by some 109s. This time Sergeant Charles Irwin was killed and his body was never recovered.

BRIAN LANE, SEPTEMBER 1940
23-year-old Sq/Ldr Brian Lane (centre) with Walter
Lawson (left) and George 'Grumpy' Unwin (right),
all of 19 Squadron. Only Unwin survived the war.

Charles Irwin had been one of a rather select band of airmen who had
started out as RAF fitters and through their ability and ambition had become
pilots. They were highly regarded for their professionalism and expertise that
had stiffened the pre-war squadrons. That same afternoon Pilot Officer
Michael Lyne was shot in the leg, yet managed to make it back across the
Channel and crash land on the beach at Walmer. In view of his wounds he
was not able to return to flying until February the following year.

Douglas Bader's No.222 Squadron was moved down to Hornchurch at
this time. On 1st June Bader shot down a Bf109 and was also credited for
damaging a Bf110. He claimed five kills in that particular dogfight. In his
next patrol he was credited with an He111 damaged and on 4th June he had
an encounter with a Do 17.

Bader had three golden rules of air combat:
1. If you have the height, you control the battle.
2. If you come out of the sun, the enemy cannot see you.
3. If you hold your fire until you are very close, you seldom miss.

Meanwhile, flying from RAF Manston, No.264 Squadron's Defiants initially met with great success when deployed over the beaches of Dunkirk. The Defiant was a two-seater fighter and the first to have a heavy power-driven independent turret with four .303 Browning machine guns, rather than conventional forward-firing armament. This was something new to the Luftwaffe and when their pilots attacked from behind in the conventional way, they suddenly found that they were flying into a concentrated hail of fire from the rear turret.

During this time their advantage enabled No.264 Squadron to claim 56 victories. Inevitably once the Luftwaffe pilots realised what was happening, attacking tactics changed and No.264's losses began to mount. The squadron ended up by losing 14 of its own aircraft and as a result, by August 1940 the Defiants had been withdrawn from daylight operations.

During the evacuation, three sorties a day had been quite normal for the fighter pilots but by 4th June it was all over. The last of the troops had been brought to safety and members of No.222 Squadron, including Tim Vigors, took part in one last patrol over Dunkirk. He described the town and its surroundings as a Dante's Inferno with fuel stores burning and vast clouds of smoke billowing into the air.

Of the 261 Hurricanes that had originally been dispatched to fly from French airfields, only 66 returned and some of these were so badly damaged that they had to be scrapped. During the Dunkirk operation Fighter Command had lost 106 fighters and more than 80 pilots had been killed.

The squadrons left Hornchurch for their home bases on 5th June. No.222 headed off for a new home at Kirton-in-Linsey in Lincolnshire, but No.19 Squadron returned to Duxford. Brian Lane described how on the flight back you could see the smoke from Dunkirk's burning fuel stores as far as London.

Group Captain Woodhall, Duxford's Station Commander was there to meet them, along with their new CO, Squadron Leader 'Tommy' Pinkham. The pilots were all looking forward to 48 hours of promised leave. Because for the past ten days they had been getting up at 3.15 in the morning and rarely getting to bed before eleven at night. Added to the fact that the days had been filled with flying and fighting, it was no wonder that they were tired. Brian Lane commented that it was like playing a strenuous game of tennis on a hot day – you don't realise how hot you are until you stop.

The first enemy bombing raid on Britain to take place after Dunkirk came on 5th June along the east coast and up as far as Norwich. The following night the raiders returned, heading into the Cambridge and Duxford area, dropping over a hundred incendiary bombs in a field about a mile and a half from the airfield. Film studio prop departments did a noble job at that time in helping to create a number of dummy airfields. These creations were often elaborate decoys, complete with phoney landing lights, hangers and aircraft . The decoy system was obviously working.

On 10th June Sqn Ldr Phillip Campbell Pinkham arrived at Duxford to formally take over as No.19 Squadron's new CO. Fifteen days later the squadron moved its Spitfires to Fowlmere and for the rest of the summer and into the autumn they moved backwards and forwards between Fowlmere and Duxford.

During June No.19 Squadron were involved in night patrols on 20 occasions. The Spitfire was not particularly suited for night fighting for various reasons. Not only did the twin banks of glowing exhausts destroy night vision, the high nose also made it difficult to see the horizon when taking off, while the narrow track undercarriage made night landings difficult.

In spite of this there was some success. The counter technique that was adopted was to wait until searchlights on the ground illuminated the enemy aircraft and then move into the attack. On the night of 18th/19th June, the Luftwaffe mounted a substantial raid, during which five Heinkel 111s were shot down.

At 1.15 am on the morning of 19th June Flying Officer Johnnie Petre intercepted and destroyed a Heinkel that had been bombing RAF Mildenhall. The Heinkel crashed in flames near Newmarket, but unfortunately the searchlight picked up Petre's aircraft and the doomed aircraft managed to get a lucky shot that hit Petre's fuel tank. Although Petre was badly burned, he managed to bail out and was taken to the General Hospital at Bury St Edmunds where he began a long process of recovery that eventually enabled him to return to the squadron some months later.

There were four men in the crew of the shot-down Heinkel; three NCOs, two of whom were sergeants and an Oberleutnant, who was equivalent in rank to an RAF Flying Officer. The officer and the two sergeants survived, but the other member of the crew was killed. The prisoners were taken to Duxford where the two sergeants turned out to be rather belligerent so were taken away and locked up. The Oberleutnant was more personable and although it was the middle of the night he was taken to the Officers Mess.

Oberleutnant Joachim von Arnim was the captain of the aircraft, although he was actually the navigator and not the pilot. This the RAF pilots found rather strange since they were used to the pilot being 'in charge'. Brian Lane in his book Spitfire relates how von Arnim 'turned out to be a really nice chap − a gentleman. Which was more than could be said for the rest of the crew!'

Von Arnim came from a German aristocratic family and Pilot Officer Peter Howard-Williams, later to be Wing Commander Howard-Williams, described how he spoke good English and apparently on the basis of Hitler's assurances was convinced that Germany would win the War.

After a few late night drinks, as daybreak approached it was decided that von Arnim needed somewhere to have a shave and freshen up. Flying Officer Leonard Haines was away at the time, so it was decided that van Arnim could use his room. When Haines returned at breakfast time he got rather a shock when he discovered a German officer in his room hard at work with his own razor.

An hour or so later Brian Lane's wife Eileen arrived at the Officer's Mess looking for her husband. Eileen and Brian Lane had only recently been married following an introduction by Gordon Sinclair. Her parents lived at Shelford, not far from Duxford.

Lane and von Arnim were talking together when she arrived and Lane was startled when von Arnim and his wife immediately recognised each other. In pre-War days she had been a very successful racing driver and had taken part in and won a number of European championships. She and the German officer knew each other from the continental racing circuits. Even in wartime it can be a small world.

The nocturnal patrols continued. On the night of 21st June about a hundred hostile aircraft descended on East Anglia, with aerodromes and towns being the principle targets. Bombs were reported in a dozen areas, including Duxford. Due to the heavy cloud the use of searchlights was futile and although air patrols were flown, no contact was made.

The Luftwaffe was making strenuous efforts to disrupt the North Sea convoys and much of the work for the 12 Group squadrons at this time

SPITFIRES
Spitfires were elegant aircraft. In all some 22,000
were built in a host of different variants and
subvariants. 19 Squadron was the first to be
equipped with Spitfires in August 1938.

involved convoy patrols. The young pilots were bursting for more action and
they found convoy patrols very frustrating and tedious.

In spite of its somewhat primitive conditions with its tents and caravans,
Duxford's satellite station at Fowlmere was now in constant use. No.19
Squadron moved there on 25th June but returned to Duxford on 3rd July
when No.264 Squadron could use Fowlmere to recuperate after the terrible
hammering that it had received in France.

On 28th June 1940 Bader was promoted to Squadron Leader and took
command of No.242 Squadron based at the newly completed RAF
Coltishall, in Norfolk. This was only 8 weeks after he had been posted to
No.222 Squadron as a flight commander. No.242 was a Hawker Hurricane
unit and Bader asked Vigor to join him.

However, Vigor declined and stayed with No.222 Squadron which later returned to Hornchurch during the Battle of Britain. In October 1940 Tim Vigors was awarded the DFC and two months later was posted to Singapore where he joined No.243 Squadron as a flight commander. His final tally of 'kills' by the end of the war was 12½.

He and Bader actually came together again some years later. By this time the war had ended and after Vigors had returned from the Far East he became one of Bader's station commanders in the North Weald sector of 11 Group. He retired from the RAF in 1946, by which time he had reached the rank of Wing Commander.

★★★

Over Dunkirk the RAF had discovered the destructive power of the cannon-equipped Bf109s, particularly when compared with the effects of the standard eight .303 Browning machine guns that were mounted in the wings of the Spitfires and Hurricanes.

The .303 guns, although widely used and of proven reliability, were really a World War I weapon. Pilots found that it took a lot of their little bullets to knock down a German bomber. In July No.19 Squadron was re-equipped with Spitfire Mk IBs that had two 20mm Hispano cannons instead of the eight .303s. These weapons packed a really big punch and they could blow apart an attacked aircraft. No.19 Squadron had been chosen to trial them under combat conditions.

It was clear that the new armament would require a change to combat techniques. Although the cannons had an increased range, destructive power and accuracy, they carried only 60 rounds. This only gave a five to six second fire period, making defence against other fighter aircraft very difficult. There was some scepticism about the benefits of changing and even after canons came into wider use a number of pilots, including Douglas Bader, continued to prefer the old eight .303 configuration.

Unfortunately it was soon found that the new weapons were very unreliable and stoppages were frequent. The problem was that the wings of the Spitfire were very thin and so the cannons had to be placed on their sides to accommodate them. As a result they kept overheating and jamming the drum feeds. Sometimes they would fire one shot before jamming or one cannon would jam and the other would not, which greatly affected the stability of the aircraft and the pilot's ability to aim.

DEFIANT

The Boulton Paul Defiants were two-seater fighters
with a heavy rear turret that had four .303
Browning machine guns. Unfortunately there was
no forward-facing armament. Initially they scored
great success, until the enemy discovered their major
weakness.

With the enemy now at the Channel coast and with invasion expected at
any time, the RAF needed all available aircraft with every squadron fully
operational. Unreliable armament was obviously a very serious problem and
reliability was of critical concern.

Meanwhile RAF Duxford was placed on high alert and made ready for
what was to come.

The Battle of Britain Begins

The RAF had learnt some important lessons from the fighting over Dunkirk. The RAF was introducing new tactics based on the Luftwaffe system of looser formations, but these had still not been fully adopted by the opening phase of what came to be called the Battle of Britain. As a result many of the most experienced and senior pilots, to whom the discipline of the old procedures came as second nature, were among the first to be shot down.

Although 10th July is the accepted date as the start of the Battle, the Luftwaffe had actually started air activity over Britain in early June, shortly after the completion of the Dunkirk evacuation.

By mid-July No.19 Squadron pilots were still trying to sort out the problems with the jamming cannons on their Spitfire Mk IBs and as a result when the Battle of Britain began the squadron was still far from ready.

On 10th July a new squadron, No.310, was formed at Duxford from Czech pilots who had managed to escape from France. It was equipped with Hurricane Mk1 fighters, although these did not begin to arrive until 18th July. This was the first RAF squadron to be crewed by foreign nationals being led jointly by British and Czech COs; Squadron Leader Douglas Blackwood and Squadron Leader Alexander (Sasha) Hess. A number of additional experienced officers, including Gordon Sinclair, also joined the new squadron. The squadron was ready in record time and began operations on 18th August, going on to claim 37½ victories in the Battle of Britain.

With mainland Europe now in German hands the enemy's next step was to take care of Britain, but this would require a significant maritime invasion and the German High Command held the view that in order for this invasion to succeed, the Luftwaffe needed to achieve air supremacy.

On 16th July Hitler issued *Directive 16 – To Eliminate the English Motherland.*

"As England, in spite of the hopelessness of her military position, has so far shown herself unwilling to come to any compromise, I have decided to begin to prepare for, and if necessary carry out, an invasion of England ... if necessary the island will be occupied."

Hitler's proposal was for "a surprise crossing on a broad front extending approximately from Ramsgate to a point west of the Isle of Wight." German troops in Holland were encouraged to think that there might still be an invasion of the East Coast between the Wash and Harwich. This was precisely where the British defence chiefs expected it to come.

SPITFIRES FLYING
Initially RAF aircraft flew and attacked in tight formations. Pilots often had to concentrate more on staying in formation than in keeping an eye out for the enemy. Many pilots were shot down before this policy changed. These aircraft are from No.611 Squadron.

LEIGH-MALLORY

Trafford Leigh-Mallory was controller of 12 Group, of which Duxford was part. He supported Douglas Bader's view that it was better to attack the enemy in large wings, rather than in the smaller groups favoured by Keith Park, controller of 11 Group.

Before the invasion could take place Hitler continued,

"The English air force must have been beaten down to such an extent morally and in actual fact that it can no longer muster any power of attack worth mentioning against the German crossing."

Göring decided to take personal control of the elimination of the RAF and had his private train brought to Calais. His strategy was to bomb the RAF airfields and use the Luftwaffe fighters to deal with any retaliation that might result.

He was confident that British fighter defences in southern England could be destroyed within four days. The rest of the RAF would take a little longer, but from two to four weeks was his estimate. After all, he had a vast armada of 963 fighters, 998 bombers and 316 dive bombers.

The RAF mounted constant day and night patrols and there were many scrambles leading to skirmishes off the East Coast. Although Duxford was part of 12 Group, tasked with defending the Midlands, it could be called in to help 11 Group in the defence of London and the South East during times of maximum effort. Although initially this hardly ever happened.

11 Group covered the North Sea as far north as Lowestoft, while 12 Group

covered the area between Lowestoft and a few miles north of the Humber Estuary. Being so far south, when Duxford squadrons took part in these patrols they usually moved up to Horsham St Faiths near Norwich so as to be closer to their operating area.

In the absence of real combat, all that 11 Group could do was practice. Practice could also be a risky business, as on 13th July No.19 Squadron lost one of its pilots, Sgt Raymond Birch flying Spitfire R6688. It was during dogfight practice at seven in the evening and during a steep turn the plane stalled and crashed into the ground, catching fire and killing its pilot. Sgt Birch's grave is also in the churchyard at Whittlesford. He had been a gifted contributor to Punch and an obituary notice later appeared in the magazine.

On 6th August RAF Duxford was visited by a number of Czech dignitaries. These included the President in Exile, Dr Eduard Benes, and the head of the Czech Air Force who came to see No.310 Squadron, although the squadron was not yet fully operational. Air Vice-Marshal Trafford Leigh-Mallory, the Air Officer Commanding Number 12 Group, accompanied the visitors. Dr Benes addressed the Czech airman, took the salute and watched a display of No.310 Squadron's aerobatics.

8th August was the day that marked the first intensive air operations and the heavy fighting brought correspondingly heavy losses. Much of this activity still centred on Channel convoys, so there was little 12 Group involvement.

On 11th August a new Spitfire was delivered to No.19 Squadron that had two cannons and four machine guns. Squadron Leader Pinkham spent over an hour test flying the new aircraft and reported that he felt this armament to be 'the right combination'. Despite the squadron's diary commenting that although this might be a step in the right direction, another step in the same direction would be to re-equip the squadron with the old eight-gun machines that the pilots favoured.

There was a great deal of to and fro activity at this time as the Germans were preparing for Operation Sealion - the invasion of Britain - on the other side of the Channel. Several 12 Group squadrons were regularly brought down to Duxford to be in readiness if required, although they also continued to operate from their home bases. Two of these were No.303 (Polish) Squadron, based at RAF Leconfield near Hull and Bader's squadron, No.242, based at RAF Coltishall, nine miles NNE of Norwich. The regular sweeps over the North Sea brought a number of successful engagements, but the pilots were still crying out for more action.

13th August had been designated 'Eagle Day' by the Germans. This was the day in which the German bomber fleets were to destroy the RAF on the ground. By dusk the Luftwaffe had failed to achieve its objective. The fierce fighting was to continue and there was no respite for the hard-pressed squadrons of 11 Group. Meanwhile frustration ruled the squadrons of 12 Group, particularly those in the Duxford sector who were within striking distance of the action but were never called into action.

Friction began to grow between the controllers of both Groups. Understandably the 11 Group Controller committed his own squadrons first and then called upon 12 Group to provide reinforcements. One of the problems was that Leigh-Mallory, the 12 Group Controller believed in the benefit of first grouping his squadrons into a "big wing" in order to attack with more force. This led to criticisms that by the time the 12 Group squadrons got into the "big wing" formation and arrived in the combat zone, the Germans had gone home. Countering this, 12 Group squadrons often complained that they were not called early enough to give them an appropriate amount of time to reach their destination.

A good example occurred on 15th August when 25 Bf110s attacked RAF Martlesham Heath and No.19 Squadron was called on to assist. The Bf110s had arrived completely undetected and only three of Martlesham's Hurricanes had managed to get airborne before they arrived. As one of the No.19 Squadron pilots pointed out, with Martlesham being 60 miles from Fowlmere and the best speed that the Spitfires could offer being about 300 mph, the squadron could not achieve the impossible.

On 15th August the Luftwaffe flew 801 bomber and 1,149 fighter sorties and despite their numerical strength, it proved to have been a disastrous day for them. Their total losses were given as 75, although this could have been as many as 100. The day became known throughout the Luftwaffe as 'Black Thursday'. There was much resentment among the 12 Group pilots that although the day had involved a considerable amount of action, their involvement had been so limited.

The following day, as they were flying back from Coltishall, seven of No.19 Squadron's pilots met a large force of enemy aircraft off Harwich and although three Bf110s were shot down, with another one listed as 'probable', six of the seven Spitfires involved had cannon stoppages. That night 220 high explosive bombs were dropped not far from Duxford but caused no significant damage.

On the afternoon of 24th August 12 Group was called up to assist 11 Group over North Weald and Hornchurch and three squadrons were dispatched. No.66 Squadron had flown its Spitfires down from Coltishall and together with No.19 Squadron and the now operational No.310 Squadron an attempt was made to group the squadrons into a "big wing". This configuration took time so when they finally reached North Weald most of the action was over. Only No.19 Squadron with their cannon armed Mk IB Spitfires made contact, but once again the guns jammed and only two Bf110s were destroyed.

No.19 Squadron moved to Fowlmere again later the same day. At Fowlmere there had been some marked progress since their previous stay, made most obvious by the number of Nissen huts increasing from two to six. It was reported in the squadron diary that:"The irrepressible Plt Off Howard-Williams re-started his excellent bar".

On 26th August the three squadrons were in action again, this time with the addition of No.229 Squadron who had flown its Hurricanes down from RAF Wittering. At this time the squadrons were still acting independently.

BENTLEY PRIORY CONTROL ROOM
From the Control Room at Fighter Command HQ at Bentley Priory Hugh Dowding, Fighter Command C in C was able to monitor attack and defence. He was later criticised for not pushing for greater co-operation between 11 and 12 Groups.

At 3.45 pm Sqn Ldr Douglas Blackwood, the No.310 CO, spotted a dozen or so Dornier 215s. Although his aircraft was fitted with a VHF radio, none of the other 11 aircraft in the squadron was similarly equipped, so he was not able to issue any orders.

He attacked one Dornier from the rear and met with a hail of fire. He backed away, but smelt burning. Soon after that his starboard wing tank burst into flames. Blackwood bailed out and landed in a stubble field, thankfully living to fight another day. One of the Czech pilots, Sgt Edward Prchal of No.310 Squadron was also shot down and although he was slightly wounded, he too survived. Thus on the very first mission where No.310 Squadron saw action it had come very close to losing both its CO and one of its other pilots.

On 28th August, No.611 Squadron made the 30-minute trip from its base at RAF Digby down to Duxford where it was to stay at readiness throughout the day before flying back in the evening. It was No.611 Squadron that had been at Duxford for its summer camp at the outbreak of war.

On 29th August, a second Czech squadron, No.312 was formed at Duxford. This also flew Hurricane Mk 1s.

The 12 Group pilots were still champing at the bit for some 'real' action as they had been for several weeks. It irritated them that the pilots of 11 Group were getting all the action and glory while they seemed to spend most of their time on tedious patrols where nothing much ever seemed to happen.

On Friday 30th August Bader's squadron got their wish, although it began as yet another frustrating day. Early in the morning the squadron received a call to fly down to Duxford from their home base a Coltishall. This was not exactly action, but at least it was closer to the action.

However, half way to Duxford a message was received ordering them to return to Coltishall. Bader was furious. He knew that for the first time the Luftwaffe was attacking with everything that it had and that by mid-morning Park's 11 Group was stretched to the limit and had all of its forces in the air.

As the day dragged on Bader could not understand why No.242 Squadron was not being called to assist. Then at 4.45 pm the phone rang and the call came to fly down to North Weald. Once airborne Bader called up Duxford operations and was told that seventy-plus 'bandits' were approaching North Weald at 15,000 feet.

Bader calculated that it would take him about 15 minutes to reach the critical point. Nonetheless if he stuck to the heading that he had been given and the enemy were where they were supposed to be, they would have the sun behind them and it would be very difficult to intercept. In the event, he positioned his aircraft in an ideal attacking position, about 15-20 miles up-sun of the target and in a completely different position to where he was being directed by the 11 Group controller.

Suddenly they encountered a huge enemy force flying in an easterly direction. Bader counted fourteen blocks of six bombers, with thirty Bf110 fighters behind and above. Bader's ten Hurricanes looked set to take on more than 100 enemy aircraft.

He led his squadron to the attack and a furious dogfight ensued resulting in a victory that saw the enemy formation broken up and the aircraft retreat in disarray. Bader's squadron claimed twelve victories and three probables, although later investigation put the true number of those destroyed at only four. However, Bader's actions seemed to confirm the value of the "big wing", and this was not forgotten by those who mattered, particularly Leigh-Mallory.

The following day, Saturday 31st August, dawned a gloriously warm summer day, disturbed at ten past eight by the air raid sirens wailing over Essex and towards Duxford. Ten minutes later came the distant rumbling of the AA guns at Debden, followed a few minutes later by the mixed batteries at Duxford and Thriplow. Today the airfields of North Weald, Duxford and Debden were the main targets. At Debden a formation of Dornier Do17s dropped about a hundred high-explosive bombs and incendiaries, with the sick quarters and barrack blocks both receiving direct hits.

Meanwhile the remaining Dorniers, escorted by a group of Messerschmitt Bf110s, were heading towards Duxford. This could have been a disaster because it was early in the morning and so there were no 12 Group fighters at readiness. Luckily the enemy aircraft were met by a hail of AA fire of such ferocity that they were driven off course.

It was 11 Group's No.111 Squadron that was patrolling nearby and managed to intercept the German aircraft, shooting down a Do17Z and a Bf110. The German bombers became disorganised and dropped most of their bombs close to the nearby villages of Shelford, Shepreth and Harston.

After No.19 Squadron managed to get airborne from Fowlmere they gave chase, but their failing cannons proved to be their undoing, with four of the Spitfires being shot down for only one Bf110 in return.

Piloting one of the Spitfires was Flying Officer James Coward who was flying the cannon and machine gun armed Spitfire that was usually flown by

Squadron Leader Pinkham. He had been on the point of firing at the Dornier bomber when he was hit in the leg by a cannon shell. He looked down and saw his foot hanging loose, but continued to open fire when his cannons jammed. He was still heading for the Dornier and the top of his Spitfire grazed the bomber's underside. The hood of the Spitfire was ripped off and his aircraft began to spiral to the ground out of control.

Coward bailed out at 22,000 feet. From that height he calculated that it would take him somewhere around a quarter of an hour to reach the ground and with a leg that was so badly injured he feared that he would bleed to death before he got that far. As a desperate measure he used the radio wire from his helmet to improvise a tourniquet. He landed about 4 miles north of Duxford on what is now the A505 and was taken to Addenbrooke's Hospital in Cambridge where his leg was amputated below the knee. James Coward survived the War to become an Air Commodore, later retiring to Australia.

Perhaps the most distressing loss of the day involved Pilot Officer Ray Aeberhardt. He had been hit but managed to get his damaged aircraft R6912 back to Fowlmere. While he was attempting to land without flaps the aircraft tipped up onto its nose, turned upside down and caught fire with Aeberhardt trapped underneath. Since Fowlmere had only the most basic fire fighting facilities all anyone could do was to stand helplessly by and watch the blaze. P/O Aeberhardt was only 19 and the youngest man in the squadron. Once again his is among the graves in Whittlesford Churchyard.

While No.19 Squadron were in the air Bader's No.242 Squadron were brought down from Coltishall to cover the Duxford Sector, but saw no action.

No.310 Squadron got its first taste of combat just after lunch the same day when it was scrambled to patrol Hornchurch at 10,000 feet. No.310 was one of the Czech squadrons and was being led on this occasion by Flight Lieutenant Gordon Sinclair. Whilst patrolling they encountered a force of 15 Dornier 215s escorted by a number of Bf110s and Bf109s. In the ensuing action four Dorniers and one Bf109 were claimed to have been shot down, with a further two damaged. Two Hurricanes were lost, but fortunately one pilot was saved.

No.611 Squadron had flown down from Digby and by the time it returned that evening, three patrols had been completed, including one over Duxford, but like Bader's squadron, no interceptions were made.

After the fight on 31st August it was clear that the problem with No.19 Squadron's jamming cannons was far from being resolved and Flight

Lieutenant Lane made representations to Squadron Leader Pinkham on behalf of the pilots.

The following day Squadron Leader Pinkham reported to Group Captain Woodhall pointing out that it was unfair to expect pilots to attack large enemy formations with unreliable armament. He went on to suggest that until the problems had been eliminated the squadron should be re-equipped with Spitfires armed with Browning guns.

Woodhall was a veteran of the Kaiser's War and was widely respected by all. He sported a monocle and was affectionately known to everyone as 'Woody'. He supported No.19 Squadron's request and wrote a strong letter of support to HQ 12 Group.

However, it was announced on 2nd September that a decision had been made to move the squadron out of the battle area and send it to RAF Digby, with its place at Fowlmere being taken by No.611 Squadron flying machine-gun equipped Spitfires. No.19 Squadron regarded this as being most unfair, believing that they were being penalised simply because of their unreliable armament.

DINGHY RESCUE

Pilots of both sides had a great fear of being shot down in the Channel. RAF fighter pilots did not have dinghies and had to rely solely on their lifejacket to stay afloat. Most of the pilots who landed in the sea simply vanished without trace. Only the lucky ones got rescued.

HEINKELL HEIII BOMBING
Perhaps the best-recognised German bomber due to
the distinctive, extensively glazed, bullet-shaped
"greenhouse" nose of later versions, the Heinkel
was the most numerous and the primary *Luftwaffe*
bomber during the early stages of World War II.

On 3rd September No.19 Squadron joined with No.310 Squadron in
claiming eight enemy aircraft destroyed after intercepting a large Luftwaffe
force that had just bombed North Weald, but during the action Sq/Ldr
Pinkham yet again suffered a jammed cannon.

When the squadron got back to Fowlmere they found a surprise visitor
waiting for them. The future Air Vice-Marshal Johnny Johnson was at that
time a lowly Pilot Officer with No.19 Squadron. He only had 23 hours flying
Spitfires and was deemed to be too inexperienced and too much of a liability
for 'ops'. He described how that afternoon a small aircraft had landed on the
grass at Fowlmere and 'the sparse, unsmiling Dowding' had stepped out. The

Commander in Chief (C-in-C) of Fighter Command had come to see for himself and decide whether or not to take No.19 Squadron out of the line.

No.19 Squadron's argument must have been convincing, because the instruction to transfer to RAF Digby was cancelled and the squadron got its replacement Spitfires by the end of the week. No.611 Squadron returned to RAF Digby.

By now Göring sensed that Hitler was running out of patience and that a new effort was required by the Luftwaffe to restore confidence. German intelligence assured him that Fighter Command was running out of aircraft and that its bases around London lay in ruins. What better time to launch an all-out attack on London. Hitler, furious at the RAF's continued attacks on Berlin was only too ready to give his approval.

All day on the 3rd September No.242 Squadron stayed at Coltishall and saw no action. The following day it continued to operate from Coltishall while No.611 remained at Digby. From Duxford both No.310 and No.19 Squadrons made fruitless patrols.

On 5th September both No.242 and No.611 came down to Duxford and Sq/Ldr Pinkham led No.19 Squadron over Hornchurch where they encountered a large enemy force of 40 Dornier 17s, escorted by 40 Bf109s. The bombers maintained their formation and in a fight over the Thames Estuary, at 10.15 am Sqn Ldr Pinkham's Spitfire P9422 was caught in the crossfire of three enemy aircraft and it was believed that it was also hit by a Bf109. His was one of 22 RAF fighters that were lost that morning.

Pinkham was badly wounded in the chin, chest and hip. He attempted to bail out, but perhaps because of his wounds he did not leave the cockpit until he was too close to the ground, and sadly he was killed.

While this had been going on, Pilot Officer Johnny Johnson and two other young pilots were back at base. Not being allowed to fly operationally they had been spending their time on humdrum ground-based duties and running errands for more senior officers. Late that morning they were called to the office of the adjutant, Flying Officer J Russell Budd.

Johnson later described the meeting.

"The Squadron Adjutant sent for us. 'You chaps are to report to No.616 at Coltishall at once. They've just been pulled out of the front line and will have time to train their new pilots. It's probably the best thing. You can see what the form is here. We must have experienced pilots who can take their place in the squadron.'

Air Vice-Marshal, Johnnie Johnson, 616 Sqn, 38 Victories.

JOHNNY JOHNSON

In mid-1940 the future Air Vice-Marshal Johnny Johnson was a young Pilot Officer at Duxford with 19 Squadron. He was deemed to be too inexperienced for operations and was posted to 616 Squadron at Coltishall to gain more experience. He went on to become the RAF's highest scoring pilot.

The phone rang and the Adjutant listened for a few moments before he slowly replaced the receiver. 'They've found the CO. Probably dead when he crashed.' For a moment he brooded. He looked up.

'Well, good luck with No.616.'"

There was no time to grieve.

Sq/Ldr Phillip Pinkham had been another career officer. He joined the RAF in 1935 and after initially serving with 17 Squadron flying biplanes he joined the Meteorological Flight based at RAF Mildenhall. Reliable meteorological date was of vital importance, but for the pilots of the flight this was often highly dangerous work, requiring great technical skill since aircraft would be taking off in conditions that would not normally be considered suitable for flying.

In January 1940 Pinkham took command of the Air Fighting School at RAF St Athan, where he was responsible for training pilots to fly Hurricanes. His command of No.19 Squadron had lasted for just under three months, after the previous CO had been lost during the Dunkirk evacuation.

In a letter to Phillip Pinkham's parents Air Vice-Marshal Leigh-Mallory wrote that he felt that the service had lost a very promising young officer. He was 25 at the time of his death and he is buried in the churchyard of St Andrew's Church Kingsbury near his parents' home in Wembley, Middlesex.

His funeral took place on the Tuesday after his death and as the coffin, draped with the RAF ensign, was carried into the church the air-raid sirens began to wail. The vicar announced that since the church was not an air raid shelter, and in accordance with the Bishop's instructions he had to invite those who wished to leave to take cover. Nobody left and the service continued. As it was drawing to its conclusion the sound of the 'all clear' was clearly heard by everyone in the congregation.

A collection was started in memory of 'Tommy' Pinkham and some time later a Spitfire known as the *Borough of Willesden* was presented to the RAF.

★★★

23-year-old Flt Lt Brian Lane was now promoted in Pinkham's place making him No.19 Squadron's fourth CO in nine months. Sandy, as he was often known, was a popular member of the squadron who had already been acting CO earlier in the year following the loss of Pinkham's predecessor.

Shortly after the Battle of Britain he wrote a memoir, *'Spitfire!'*. This was published just before his death, but wartime censorship restrictions prevented the identity of any people or locations. The name of the author also had to be disguised and the book was credited to 'B. J. Ellan'.

Brian Lane's tenure as CO was to last a little longer than the recent average, but his life was also to be cut short on 13th December 1942. During a sweep over Holland his elderly Spitfire was jumped by a much faster FW190. Nobody saw him go down and it was assumed that his aircraft vanished in the North Sea.

His name is listed on the Runnymede RAF Memorial among the 20,331 RAF personnel who were lost during operations from bases in the United Kingdom and North and Western Europe and who have no known grave. Like Pinkham, Sandy Lane was 25 when he was killed.

★★★

On Thursday 5th September 1940, during the evening at their base at Fowlmere, the members of No.19 Squadron had little time to mourn the loss of their leader Tommy Pinkham because the following day they were to become part of what was to become the new 'Duxford Wing'.

The
Duxford
Wing

T he 6th September proved to be a busy day. No.611 Squadron flew down to Fowlmere to cover for No.19 Squadron while they exchanged their cannon armed Spitfires for the more conventional 8 machine gun variety. Since most of these had been drawn from Operational Training Units they were described as 'rather worn', but the pilots were delighted with them.

On the same day Squadron Leader Lane was informed that until further notice No.19 Squadron would fly as part of a wing led by Squadron Leader Bader. Bader's Hurricanes would move down to Duxford from Coltishall, but No.19 Squadron would continue to operate from Fowlmere. That first day the wing carried out two patrols, but no enemy aircraft were met on either occasion.

Saturday 7th September was rather different. Just under a fortnight previously, on Sunday 25th August, due to a navigational error a German plane had dropped some bombs on London. The RAF had immediately taken up the challenge and flown several raids over Berlin. Göring was humiliated because he had always maintained that this would never happen and as a result he decided to personally command the assault on London. Every available aircraft was to be used, with more bombers than ever before.

Meanwhile, at Fighter Command HQ the day began very much as it had for the past few weeks. The three Duxford squadrons were scrambled at 11.15 am, but nothing was seen. Then, just before 4.00 pm, the first radar reports came through that prompted Bentley Priory to alert 11 Group.

An air armada of 965 aircraft was building up over the French coast. There were 348 bombers and 617 fighters. This vast formation, about 20 miles wide and one and a half miles high was stacked in layers from 14,000 to 20,000 feet. At 4.16 pm the Observer Corps reported 'many hundreds of aircraft' heading towards the coast.

At 4.17 eleven fighter squadrons were ordered to scramble and six minutes later all the remaining 11 Group squadrons were brought to readiness. By

4.30 pm every squadron in the London area was in the air, bringing the total to 23 squadrons. Even so, calls went out to 10 and 12 Groups to ask them to stand by to help.

Dowding knew that if his fighter airfields were once again the targets of this major force, they could be completely wiped out and the Luftwaffe may soon dominate the air space, making an invasion a certainty rather than a possibility.

LONDON BOMBED
What became known in London as the "Blitz" began on 7th September 1940, when the Luftwaffe sent 965 aircraft, including 348 bombers, to attack the city. The raid caused enormous destruction, beginning late in the afternoon and lasting until after dark.

Very soon it became clear that this was no ordinary raid. Once they had crossed the coast the enemy aircraft started changing direction, criss-crossing flight paths and making it very difficult for those on the ground to determine their intentions. Eventually it became clear that this time the target was London and not the airfields. Two waves, followed later by a third, came from different directions and began to attack the East End of London.

This came as a great surprise, because the squadrons had been patrolling the airfields in the belief that as usual these would be the targets. Although 23 squadrons were already airborne, only a few were able to intercept the bombers before they reached the city. As usual, Bader was desperately ready to go, but had to wait for the call from 11 Group. Eventually assistance was requested and under Bader's leadership the Duxford wing took off at 4.45 pm and headed in the direction of North Weald, about 25 miles to the south.

Their information was that 100 enemy aircraft were approaching from the east and that they would be flying at 10,000 feet. However, when the Duxford wing arrived, they realised that the German aircraft were actually 10,000 feet higher than expected. This meant that the RAF aircraft had no height advantage and they would be attacking the bombers with the Messerschmitts above them and in the eye of the sun. Bader was frustrated that he had not been called to scramble earlier since he believed that this would have enabled him to get his wing into a more favourable position.

Rather than head for Maidstone as he had originally been directed, Bader led the Wing towards the Isle of Sheppey. The bulk of the fighting took place over the Thames Estuary and was fast and furious. With No.19 Squadron's Spitfires about 3,000 feet above were No.242 and No.310 Squadrons in their Hurricanes.

As the Hurricane squadrons were climbing, they got 'bounced' by 60 Bf109s. Bader's Hurricane, P3061, was badly damaged and it was said that his cockpit was full of bullets. Sub-Lieutenant Dickie Cork, also of No.242 was slightly injured. One of No.242's Canadian pilots, 25-year-old Pilot Officer John Benzie from Winnipeg disappeared without trace, so presumably his aircraft crashed into the Thames Estuary. His name is among those on the Runnymede Memorial.

No.310 Squadron also lost two aircraft. Sgt I Koukal, one of the Czech pilots narrowly escaped death when he managed to bail out just before his Hurricane V7437 crashed near Capel Fleet. Although he was grievously burned and was admitted to hospital. Pilot Officer Goth flying

Hurricane V6643 managed to force land at Whitman's Farm following combat over Southend.

The final tally for the engagement was No.242 Squadron destroyed 10 confirmed, with 2 probables and 3 damaged; No.310 Squadron had 5 destroyed with 3 probables and 3 damaged; and No.19 Squadron destroyed 5 of the enemy. Unfortunately in the heat of battle it was always difficult to make an accurate tally and these figures were later revealed to have been gross overestimations.

This was the first day of what came to be known as 'the Blitz' leaving parts of East London and the docks were wrecked. There was complete devastation with unexploded and delayed action bombs everywhere. Thousands were made homeless and it was estimated that during that day and the following night some 430 civilians were killed with a further 1,600 seriously injured.

As the fires burned the Luftwaffe continued to rain down bombs. The raid continued from 8.10 pm, through the night until 4.30 am. Nobody realised at the time that this was only the first of 77 consecutive nights of bombing, with just one night's break due to bad weather.

On 8th September 13 Spitfires from No.611 Squadron flew down to join No.19 Squadron in Fowlmere and No.242 Squadron flew down from Coltishall again to join No.310 Squadron at Duxford. As it turned out 12 Group's assistance was not required that day and its aircraft stayed on the ground.

On 9th September the Luftwaffe repeated what it had done two days previously and just after 4.00 pm sent over two waves in quick succession. Fighter forces ranging ahead and on the flanks of the bomber formations. One raid was met over Kent and the enemy aircraft scattered after jettisoning their bombs.

As usual the Duxford squadrons were impatiently waiting and in the late afternoon the Wing was scrambled and told to patrol over North Weald and Hornchurch at 20,000 feet. Once Bader was up in the air he decided otherwise and climbed to 22,000 feet heading for Staines where at about 5.40 pm he saw a large enemy force approximately 15 miles to the south west.

Once again he had the same three squadrons as two days before, No.242, No.310 and No.19; although this time he only had 33 fighters instead of 34. The enemy force consisted of about 75 Do 215s, accompanied by about 150 Bf110s and Bf109s.

There was an intense air battle and claims at the end of the day were that No.242 Squadron destroyed eleven enemy aircraft, No.310 Squadron destroyed three, with three probables and one damaged, while No.19 Squadron destroyed six with one probable and one damaged.

This victory was not without cost. Two of No.19 Squadron's Spitfires were damaged and No.242 lost two Hurricanes. Although Sgt R W Lonsdale parachuted to safety, P/O Kirkpatrick Sclanders, one of the Canadian pilots died after crash landing his Hurricane P3087 near Rye. Pilot Officer Rypl of No.310 Squadron also crash landed but he was unhurt. No.310 Squadron did lose two of its Hurricanes when in the middle of an attack on a Dornier bomber. R4084 piloted by F/O Gordon Sinclair was in collision with P3888 piloted by P/O John Boulton and a Bf110 from 9/ZG76. This is credited as being the biggest mid-air collision of the Battle of Britain.

Sinclair managed to bail out safely, but Boulton was killed. On the opposing side, the German pilot, Leutnant Ostermüncher, fell without his parachute opening and his gunner was found dead in the burnt out wreckage. After a descent that lasted for nearly 13 minutes, Sinclair eventually landed in a wood just off the Purley Way in Coulsden. By a strange coincidence the first person on the scene was Lieutenant G D Cooper of the Irish Guards, who was an old school friend of Sinclair's.

Cooper had had been watching the scene unfold and took Sinclair back to the Guards officers' mess at Caterham. Unfortunately since Sinclair was wearing his flying clothes over his pyjamas he was considered to be improperly dressed and was not allowed in to dine.

By now the remaining aircraft in the Duxford group were running short of fuel and they scattered as they landed at various 11 Group airfields. Until the aircraft were able to return to Duxford they were unable to operate as a Wing at Readiness.

LONDON BURNS

London's Dockland was a prime target. 1.5 million tons of timber was set alight at Surrey Docks and when the Tate and Lyle sugar refinery was hit, sheets of molten sugar covered the river. Whole areas had to be abandoned to burn themselves out.

In spite of it being a successful encounter, Bader had led the Wing some distance from where they had been told to patrol. This action did not help Park's growing aggravation that 12 Group squadrons were not giving him the support that he was asking for. As 'Johnny' Johnson, later commented, '...fortunately for Bader neither North Weald nor Hornchurch was attacked, otherwise Park might have lodged an official complaint with Dowding.'

The statistics were impressive and at that time statistics were very important even if they were not accurate. On that day the Wing claimed 20 enemy aircraft destroyed for the loss of four Hurricanes. Again this was an inflated figure since the Luftwaffe's total loss for the day was 28.

On 10th September No.242 Squadron remained at Coltishall while Bader flew up to 12 Group HQ to meet with Leigh-Mallory in order to discuss the Wing's progress to date and consider future possibilities. Bader requested even more fighters to be absorbed into his big wing.

Once again No.611 Squadron flew down to Fowlmere to join No.19 Squadron and this time it was joined by 14 Spitfires of No.74 Squadron, known as the Tiger Squadron, that had flown down from Coltishall to stand-in for No.242 Squadron. The South African Sq/Ldr Adolph G Malan was the leader of No.74 Squadron and having begun his adult life in the merchant navy was universally known as 'Sailor'.

He had joined No.74 Squadron on 20th December 1936 and unusually he stayed with the same squadron throughout his RAF career. In January 1937 he was promoted to Pilot Officer and in August that year he was made acting Flight Commander. He was then promoted to Flight Lieutenant just before the start of the War.

No.74 squadron had seen a considerable amount of action during the Dunkirk Evacuation and as a result, on 28th June Malan had been awarded the DFC. Once the Battle of Britain got fully underway the squadron moved to Hornchurch and saw action from the very start. Milan took over command on 8th August at the height of the battle and three days later came the day that became known as 'Sailor's August the Eleventh'.

That day the order had been received at 7.20 am to intercept a hostile raid approaching Dover and the squadron participated in four separate air battles that day, resulting in the shooting down of 38 enemy aircraft. It was impossible for the squadron to keep up this hectic pace and in mid-August they were were moved to RAF Wittering for a short rest before moving again to Kirton-in-Lindsey and then to Coltishall.

Malan was a strict disciplinarian who expected the best of his men at all times. He was acknowledged as being a great tactician and had developed a set of rules for fighter pilots. In time this found its way throughout Fighter Command and eventually could be found tacked to the wall in most RAF stations.

1. Wait until you see the whites of his eyes. Fire short bursts of one or two seconds only when your sights are definitely 'ON'.

2. Whilst shooting think of nothing else, brace the whole of your body: have both hands on the stick: concentrate on your ring sight.

3. Always keep a sharp lookout. "Keep your finger out."

4. Height gives you the initiative.

5. Always turn and face the attack.

BADER AND NOSE ART

Sq Ldr Bader with two of his Canadian pilots from 242 Squadron, Flt Lt G E Ball DFC on the left of the picture and P/O Willie McKnight DFC. They are admiring some unofficial nose art on one of their Hurricanes at Duxford in September 1940.

6. Make your decisions promptly. It is better to act quickly even though your tactics are not the best.

7. Never fly straight and level in the combat area for more than 30 seconds.

8. When diving to attack always leave a proportion of your formation above to act as top guard.

9. INITIATIVE, AGGRESSION, AIR DISCIPLINE and TEAMWORK are words that MEAN something in Air Fighting.

10. Go in quickly – Punch hard – Get out!

In the event there was no action on 10th September so Sq/Ldr Malan flew his Spitfires back to Coltishall. The following day No.242 Squadron again remained at Coltishall and Sq/Ldr Malan brought No.74 down to Fowlmere for a second time to join with No.19 and No.611 Squadrons to cover the Duxford Sector. This time they were also joined by a flight from No.266 Squadron that was also operating from Coltishall.

Leigh-Mallory's reinforcement policy continued with the arrival of No.302 (Polish) Squadron flying Hurricanes. This put the equivalent of three Spitfire squadrons (No.19, No/266/74 and No.611), plus two Hurricane

'SAILOR' MALAN
South African Adolf 'Sailor' Malan had been a merchant navy officer before joining 74 Squadron in 1936. Unusually he stayed with the same squadron throughout his career, taking over leadership on 8th August 1940. He was a strict disciplinarian, but was acknowledged as being a great tactician. Sketch by Cuthbert Orde.

squadrons (No.302 and No.310) at the disposal of Sector Control, meaning that there would now be some 50 to 60 fighters dispersed around Duxford and Fowlmere each day.

Late in the afternoon of 11th September Sq/Ldr Brian Lane led an all Spitfire wing made up of eight of his own squadron, plus six of No.266 Squadron, together with Malan's No.74 and McComb's No.611 Squadrons to attack a large Luftwaffe bomber formation south-east of London towards Gravesend. Together they claimed 13 enemy aircraft destroyed, with five damaged. Two Spitfires were lost and one pilot, 22-year-old Sgt Frederic Shepherd of No.611 Squadron, was killed.

On 12th September No.611 flew across to Fowlmere to join No.19 Squadron. At the same time No.242 rejoined the Wing, flying south with No.302 to join No.310 at Duxford. Intermittent rain and poor visibility led to an uneventful day before they all returned to their respective bases. The next day, Friday 13th was more or less a repeat of the previous day, although today the bad weather was accompanied by thunder. For the first time No.302 (Polish) Squadron was officially attached to Duxford. No.242 Squadron was the only squadron to fly that day and uneventfully patrolled North Weald. Also on that day No.19 Squadron received eight replacement Spitfires, all Mk IIs, plus three replacement pilots.

On Saturday 14th September the weather was showery, cloudy and locally thundery and yet the Duxford Wing still took off twice to patrol London. Although No.19, No.611, No.242, No.302 and No.310 Squadrons were all at Readiness in the Duxford Sector, in the event No.611 didn't fly on either occasion. This was No.302's first outing with the Duxford Wing but in their patrol over the London area there was no sign of the enemy.

On the way back from the first patrol inexplicably Sergeant Frantisek Marek flying Spitfire R6625 suddenly dived out of the formation and crashed near Orsett in Essex. It is thought that he suffered a failure of his oxygen system. Sgt Marek was 27 and had joined No.310 (Czech) Squadron on 6th August 1940. He had been attached to 'A' flight of No.19 Squadron since 29th August. Sgt Marek was buried in Eastbrookend Cemetery, Dagenham. On 14th September 1975, the 35th anniversary of Marek's crash, the Thameside Aviation Museum decided to excavate the remains of the aircraft. These are now displayed at the museum at Coalhouse Fort in East Tilbury.

In the afternoon of 14th September the Luftwaffe decided to risk the bad weather and send over a large number of aircraft. Once again the main target was London. One large group headed up through Kent with the other moving up the Thames Estuary. This time the Wing patrolled over Kent, but once again they made no enemy contact.

Hitler meanwhile had decided that since air superiority had not yet been achieved, he would further delay the date on which Operation Sealion, the invasion of Britain, would take place. New orders would be issued on 17th September with the operation starting ten days later.

Sunday 15th September was the day that the Battle of Britain reached its peak and it subsequently came to be celebrated annually as Battle of Britain Day. The air fighting of the previous day had generated a false sense of optimism among the Luftwaffe and the first enemy patrols arrived soon after 9.00 am. Soon after 10.30am unambiguous reports began to arrive of a massive build-up of aircraft over the Pas de Calais.

By 10.55 all of 11 Group's squadrons had been put at readiness and a request went out to 12 and 10 Groups requesting reinforcements. The first wave of the enemy's morning attack crossed the coast shortly after 11.00 am and consisted of 100 or more aircraft, closely followed by another 150. The formidable force was made up of Do17s and Do215s, escorted by twice as many Bf109s. All were positioned in a massive formation almost two miles wide and stacked up in layers between 15,000 and 26,000 feet. A furious battle raged over Kent as the aircraft made their way towards London.

The Duxford Wing was scrambled at 11.30 am. Initially made up of No.19, No.242, No.302, and No.310 Squadrons, and joined about one minute later by No.611 Squadron that had just flown down from Digby. By the time the Luftwaffe armada reached London just before midday, there were 15 squadrons of Hurricanes and 8 squadrons of Spitfires ready to meet them. Bader and his 56 fighters arrived with the sun behind them, in an ideal tactical position 3,000 feet above the bombers.

As the Wing drew nearer to the black specks, it seemed as though the whole sky was filled with aircraft. Sq/Ldr Brian Lane of No.19 Squadron said that it looked as though, '…the whole Luftwaffe was over London.' He later wrote that never before or since had he seen so many enemy aircraft in the sky at one time. There were literally hundreds of them and it was, he said, an amazing sight and one that he would remember all his life. The Wing smashed into the bombers just as they released their loads. The bombers scattered in all directions making it impossible for the dwindling number of Bf109's to protect them.

For the first time the Luftwaffe realised that they were outnumbered. Accurate bombing became out of the question as the German aircraft tried to get away. Bombs fell all over the place including two at Buckingham Palace. The fighting was intense and lasted for about an hour. During that time the Wing's 56 fighters managed to destroy 26 enemy aircraft. The Wing's only casualty was Flight Lieutenant Eric Ball from No.242 who had been shot down at 12.45 and made a forced landing, but was safe.

Once back at Duxford the pilots hardly had time to grab a bite to eat and refuel their aircraft before they were scrambled again, taking off at 2.12 pm.

EAST END BLITZ
It is estimated that during the period from July to December 1940, 2,951,000 bombs were dropped on London. This included 23,716 tons of high explosive and 2,918 tons of incendiaries. Most landed on the East End, where whole areas were completely destroyed.

The same five squadrons were involved, but after the earlier intensive fighting they could muster only 49 fighters instead of the previous 56. The clouds were eight tenths at 5,000 feet, but Bader led them through a gap and they headed south, still climbing.

This time there were 400 German fighters to protect 150 bombers. Göring had hoped that the afternoon attack would have caught the RAF on the ground, but the speed of the turn around had meant that all of the squadrons were ready. The first German wave crossed the coast near Dungeness at 2.15 pm, followed by two more at ten minute intervals.

In all, 31 RAF squadrons were in action that afternoon. Fighting all the way, the enemy aircraft reached the outskirts of London only to be faced with the biggest concentration of fighters they had yet encountered. There were ten squadrons from 11 Group, plus the five from the Duxford Wing, totalling a force of 170 fighters. When they spotted the enemy aircraft Bader realised that the Duxford aircraft were about 4,000 feet below them. This annoyed Bader, who felt that if they had only been scrambled a little earlier the Duxford Wing would have been able to gain the height advantage and therefore be better positioned.

In spite of all this, the sheer numerical strength of the Wing had the desired effect. The Luftwaffe pilots were dismayed. Their propaganda machine had assured them that Fighter Command was in its death throes, but from what they witnessed this was quite obviously not the case. The German aircraft were forced out of formation and from being the aggressors, to now simply fighting for their lives. The battle developed into a fast and furious conflict. While the morning battle had taken place over London, the afternoon battle extended from London towards the South Coast and over central Kent.

Once again accurate bomb aiming was impossible and bombs fell over a wide area as the bomber formations were scattered. That afternoon the Duxford Wing of 49 aircraft claimed to have destroyed a further 26 enemy aircraft, making a total of 52 aircraft in one day. The Wing's losses included four Hurricanes and two Spitfires, with two other aircraft badly damaged.

Sgt J Hubacek from No.310 Squadron was the first to go. He had to bail out after his Hurricane (R4087) had been in combat with a Bf109 over the Thames Estuary at 2.30 pm. He had an injured foot and was admitted to Chatham Hospital.

At 2.40 pm Fl/Lt George Powell-Sheddon, one of Bader's Flight Commanders on No.242 Squadron was shot down by a Bf109 while attacking a Do17 and when baling out dislocated his shoulder when he bounced off his Hurricane's tail.

Five minutes later came the Wing's only fatality of the day when Ft/Lt Tadeusz Chlopik, of No.302 (Polish) Squadron suffered crippling damage to his Hurricane P2954. Although he managed to bail out, he was dead when he reached the ground. At about the same time Sq/Ldr Alexander (Shasha) Hess, joint CO of No.310 (Czech) Squadron flying Hurricane R4085 was forced to bail out over the Thames Estuary. He landed safely and was unhurt, but his aircraft crashed in flames south of Billericay.

Five minutes later at 2.50, Flying Officer T D Williams of No.611 Squadron suffered severe damage to his Spitfire II P7303 after an encounter with a He111. Thankfully, he was uninjured and managed to nurse his badly disabled aircraft back to base.

At 3.00 pm, after combat action over the Channel in Spitfire R6991, Sub/Lt Arthur Blake, the Admiral of No.19 Squadron, had to make a forced landing in Kent, but was unhurt. Meanwhile at Rochford Sub/Lt R J Cork of No.242 Squadron was making a forced landing with damage to the cockpit and wings of his Hurricane P3515 following combat with a BF109.

Cork and Blake was two of 56 Fleet Air Arm pilots who took part in the Battle of Britain. They were attached to Fighter Command squadrons and although all continued to wear naval uniform, they were subject to RAF rules and discipline. Nine of them, including Arthur Blake, were killed. 'The Admiral' was from HMS Daedalus at Lee on Solent and had been attached to No.19 Squadron for nearly four months.

At five past three Sgt J Kowalski of No.302 Squadron was forced to return to base in Hurricane P3935 after it was damaged by enemy action. Whilst on the other side of the Channel Sgt J A Potter of No.19 Squadron had just been shot down after chasing a Bf109 as far as the French coast in his Spitfire X4070. He was wounded but managed to ditch in the sea and was taken prisoner.

The final casualty of the day was another pilot from No.19 Squadron, Sgt H A C Roden flying Spitfire (P9431), who managed to crash land at Fowlmere at 3.10 pm. after a fight with a Bf109. He suffered slight injuries in the process and his aircraft was a write off.

The Air Ministry announced that the total tally of German aircraft shot down on that day was 183 and this proved to be an enormous morale booster for both the RAF and the civilian population. While it was later shown that this figure was optimistically high, with the true number being 56, the loss still had a devastating effect on the Luftwaffe. On the same day Fighter Command lost 26 aircraft and 13 pilots.

In the space of 90 minutes, the Luftwaffe had been thrown into an action that involved facing 250 British fighters from 28 RAF squadrons. Being confronted with this number had a shattering effect on the German bomber crews and made nonsense of Göring's proud boast that the RAF was down to its last 50 Spitfires. For two months the Luftwaffe had experienced a very heavy loss rate convincing Hitler and Göring that the actions of 15th September would finally finish off the RAF. However, when the German bomber pilots were debriefed it became quite very evident that they had been attacked by RAF squadrons that were no longer supposed to exist.

For Fighter Command almost everything had gone right that day. The whole process, from detection by radar stations and the Observer Corps, to interception as a result of accurate direction by Group and sector commanders and finally destruction by the pilots had all functioned exactly as it was planned to do. Wreckage of German aircraft was spread across Southeast England and the Daily Express crowed that: "Göring might reflect that this is no way to run an invasion."

The following day, 16th September, the weather on both sides of the Channel was foul and Göring called a meeting. Clearly Dowding was not down to his last 50 Spitfires after all, but Göring still maintained that Fighter Command could be destroyed in four or five days. This belief was based on the greatly inflated battle-damage estimates of 15th September. On that day the Germans believed that they had destroyed 79 RAF aircraft rather than the true number of 26.

On 17th September Hitler ordered that Operation Sealion should be postponed indefinitely, although a high state of readiness should still be maintained. During that day the Duxford squadrons downed two more Bf109s.

On 18th September the Duxford Wing was back in action again. After two uneventful sorties the Wing took off for its third mission at sixteen minutes past four in the afternoon to patrol the area from Central London to Thameshaven. They were flying at a height of 19,000 to 20,000 feet when they saw two formations of German bombers approaching the first bend in the Thames near Gravesend. Each group was made up of 20 to 30 aircraft, flying along at between 15,000 and 17,000 feet and they appeared to be completely without escorts.

The Duxford wing attacked and for a while it seemed that chaos reigned as the sky was filled with aircraft flying in every direction. At the end of the engagement the Wing claimed 29 aircraft destroyed. The actual number was later said to have been four, although some sources maintain it was six, but the reality of the situation was that the Luftwaffe's total loss over England on that day was only 18 aircraft.

Although it is now known that the Wing's claims were often overstated, the claims were made in good faith and were accepted as a morale booster. Bader's adjutant Peter Macdonald, known as 'Boozy Mac' to the pilots, had been a Member of Parliament since 1924 and through his connections was able to speak to Churchill regarding the 'Big Wing' theory. This, together with the claims that were being made of the numbers of enemy aircraft shot down, helped to make people who mattered sit up and take note.

OBSERVER CORPS POST
Accurate plotting of incoming aircraft was essential to Fighter Command's defence strategy. Although radar played a vital part in this, much depended on direct observation and accurate reporting from members of the Observer Corps.

The following day No.616 Squadron replaced No.611 in the Duxford Wing. Like No.611, No.616 flew down to Duxford each day from its home base, which in this case was Kirton-in-Lindsey in Lincolnshire. No.616 had been based at Kenley during the early part of the Battle of Britain and the two weeks of fierce fighting had taken a heavy toll. On one sortie in particular the squadron had been attacked by some Bf109s and had lost seven Spitfires with two pilots killed and two injured. Over half of the squadron became casualties and on 3rd September the remaining members were moved to Coltishall to be rested before moving to a new home at Kirton-in-Lindsey.

A variety of newcomers came to No.616. A new CO had been appointed, Sq/Ldr 'Billy' Burton and fresh pilots arrived, one of whom was Pilot Officer Johnny Johnson who had transferred from No.19 Squadron. Johnny Johnson went on to score the highest number of victories against the Luftwaffe in the European war. He retired in 1966 with a rank of Air Vice Marshal.

Things were now calming down a bit for the Duxford pilots although there was still the occasional burst of action. One such occassion came on 22 September when a lone Dornier flew over Fowlmere and dropped a stick of bombs along one of the dispersal points. One Spitfire was destroyed, but apart from that no damage was done. The Dornier dived into cloud and got away.

The following day the Wing patrolled again, but without incident. This time No.19 Squadron patrolled over Duxford to guard against a similar attack. Uneventful patrols continued over the next few days. On 25 September No.302 (Polish) Squadron left Duxford reducing the wing to four squadrons: No.19, No.242, No.310 and No.616. No.19 Squadron received a number of new Spitfire Mk II fighters that had a number of improvements over the Mk IA machines that they had been using.

The last big battle for the Duxford Wing occurred on 27th September. The four squadrons had been scrambled at 11.45 am and 30 minutes later they were flying at a height of 23,000 feet over the Dover-Canterbury area when they sighted a force of Bf109s about 3,000 to 4,000 feet below them. During the fast and furious action the result was the loss of 13 Bf109s for three RAF pilots killed and one wounded. The first three British losses occurred almost immediately. At 12.20 pm Sgt David Cox of No.19 Squadron was wounded in a dogfight, but managed to crash-land his Spitfire X4237 near Wye.

At the same time Gordon Sinclair of No.310 Squadron, flying Hurricane V6608, was shot down by a Bf109 over Thanet. Although his aircraft caught fire, Sinclair was uninjured and safely bailed out, landing in the top of a tree. His plane crashed at Godmersham. Within seconds of these two casualties 26-year-old F/O Donald Smith of No.No.616 Squadron flying Spitfire R6702 was shot down by a Bf109 near to Faversham. He was seriously injured and was taken to Faversham Cottage hospital where he died the following day. He was later buried near his home in Shropshire.

Events moved swiftly and five minutes after the first incident 21-year-old Flying Officer Michael Homer DFC of No.242 Squadron was killed when his Hurricane (P2967) was shot down over Sittingbourne. His plane crashed in the garden of a cottage in Milstead. His grave is in Swanage among 15 other graves from World War II. The third fatality was to P/O Eric Burgoyne of No.19 Squadron flying Spitfire X4352. He was killed after he was shot down by a Bf109 over Canterbury and crashed at Coldred at 12.30 pm. He was 25 and his funeral also took place near his home in Berkshire.

Squadron Leader Lane had been flying one of the new Mk II Spitfires at 25,000 feet and after firing two short bursts at an enemy, the controls of his aircraft stiffened up causing his aircraft suddenly to became uncontrollable. He went into a steep dive and very soon his airspeed indicator showed that he was doing well over 400 mph and he was already down to 10,000 feet and still falling rapidly.

He considered bailing out, but thought that at such speed this would not be possible, so he made one last Herculean attempt to haul back on the control column and regain control of the aircraft. To his relief this time he was successful. Although he blacked out in the process he regained consciousness only to find that he was flying upside down. He managed to return to base where his aircraft was found to have had a misshaped rudder and a wrongly adjusted trim tab that had prevented one elevator from functioning correctly.

Meanwhile, the Duxford Wing was coming to be one of the most contentious issues of the Battle of Britain. Leigh-Mallory, commander of 12 Group, was anxious for his squadrons to have a share in some of the action. He began to advocate what came to be called 'the Big Wing' when several squadrons were sent up at the same time and attacked together. He believed in meeting force with force and shooting down as many of the enemy as possible. Leigh-Mallory had friends in high places and so he managed to get some very influential people on his side.

One of Leigh-Mallory's strongest supporters was Squadron Leader Douglas Bader of No.242 Squadron. Following his experiences over the French beaches, Bader was convinced of the merits of large formations. Leigh-Mallory welcomed his famous and vociferous new ally and recognised that this was a golden opportunity for his command to develop its profile by giving it a greater role in the battle. Dowding and 11 Group's Park considered that the suggestion was completely contrary to the carefully developed strategy and they received the idea with great coolness.

One major problem was that Park and Leigh-Mallory were incompatible

DUXFORD WAR GRAVES
A small section of the churchyard at nearby Whittlesford was set aside for the graves of RAF personnel who lost their lives at Duxford. Many of these deaths were as a result of accidents.

characters. While Park was a skilled defensive tactician and a talented fighter pilot, Leigh-Mallory was much more experienced as a staff officer and was more inclined to offensive action. Another issue was that links between 11 Group and 12 Group were not properly streamlined. Incoming raids often overlapped both Groups, but there was a lack of unified command. While Group Controllers knew what was going on in their own Group, there was no "big picture" of what was going on elsewhere. This left both Groups to operate independently and although they could request assistance of each other, nobody had the unquestioned authority to co-ordinate their efforts.

A feature of Bader's proposed plan, supported by Leigh-Mallory, was that control should be centralised from the headquarters of Fighter Command at Stanmore. Bader felt that since it was only here that the whole mass of the country was displayed, together with all the necessary technical systems and details of squadron strengths and locations.

A most unfortunate element was that the controversy spread and views became generally polarised throughout both Groups Something, according to Lucas, that had originally been conceived as a mutually supportive arrangement between two neighbouring Groups gradually blew itself up until there were two camps, either supporting Park and deriding Leigh-Mallory or vice versa.

In the aftermath of the Battle of Britain, on 17th October 1940, the Air Council held a meeting and this is where the Big Wing dispute reached its climax. Leigh-Mallory surprised everyone by taking along Douglas Bader, who was by far the most junior and inexperienced officer present.

Leigh-Mallory was a very eloquent critic of his colleague and his strategy. He boasted that he could get 5 Duxford squadrons airborne within six minutes and within 25 minutes they could be over Hornchurch. In practice, it had taken 17 minutes for the Duxford Wing to leave the ground and a further 20 minutes for them to set course from base.

Bader addressed the meeting and told them that it should be the 'chap in the air' and not the controller who should decide when, where and how to meet the enemy. This of course went completely against the whole interception system that had been so painstakingly developed by Dowding. While in some quarters this was regarded as being nothing short of heresy, as aerial combat techniques continued to develop it soon came to be realised that there were times when the 'chap in the air' was indeed better placed to make appropriate on-the-spot decisions.

It was clear that Dowding had no support from the Air Council where he had few friends. In fact Hugh Dowding was not a widely loved character. Although broadly respected by his pilots and ground crews, over the years he had crossed swords with too many important people. He had no ear for politics and distrusted most politicians. He happily spent four years preparing Fighter Command for a battle that had just been comprehensively won, but it was not his style to get involved in a political fight.

In November he was removed from command of Fighter Command and sent to the USA to represent the Ministry of Aircraft Production. Although it is probably not true, as some have said, that he was given only 24 hours notice to vacate his office at Bentley Priory, many felt that he was shamefully treated by being relieved of his Command so promptly.

At the same time Keith Park was utterly drained and exhausted, so the Air Council decided that he too should be relieved of his command. Park saw this as an insulting slight and ever after held that men were prejudiced against him. He was initially offered a job on the Air Staff, but turned this down because he saw the Air Ministry as a place of intrigue and plots, so it was decided to move him to supervise a Group in Training Command. Leigh-Mallory took over from Park as Commander of 11 Group, which somewhat rubbed salt into Park's wounded pride. Within two years Park was rejuvenated and ready to take over the defence of Malta.

Even after all this time, intense passions can still be roused regarding the merits or otherwise of the Duxford Big Wing strategy during the Battle of Britain and by the possible conspiracies in the months that followed the Battle.

All Change at Duxford

The last true mission for the Duxford Wing had been on 27th September 1940. On 28th September, No.242 and No.616 Squadrons both returned to Duxford and joined in patrols over the Thames Estuary, but no action took place. The following day the weather was so bad that nobody flew and No.616 received formal notification that it would no longer be required at Fowlmere.

On 3rd October Pilot Officer Vokes returned from the Air Fighting Development Unit at Northolt with a new Spitfire, R6889, for No.19

MOSQUITO
Late in 1941 the Air Fighting Development Unit moved into Duxford. One of the aircraft to be evaluated was the new, very fast and highly secret De Havilland Mosquito. This was found to be even faster than a Spitfire.

Squadron to test. This model was again fitted with cannons, but with a new design and it was hoped that this would prevent the jamming that had blighted the earlier version. Vokes tested the new Spitfire on the ranges at Sutton Bridge and found that the only time the guns jammed was when the aircraft was subjected to tight 'g-forces'.

The three remaining squadrons, No.19, No.242 and No.310, still regularly flew together and it was during this time that No.19 Squadron lost Sub Lieutenant Arthur Charles Blake, who had always been known as 'the Admiral'. They were flying over Kent on Tuesday 29th October and although some of the pilots saw some Bf109s in the distance, no attack was made.

The Admiral was acting as weaver at the Bf109s picked him off in a surprise attack. He crashed at 5.15 pm near Chelmsford and is buried in St Mary's churchyard at Langley near Slough.

Three other Fleet Air Arm pilots were at Duxford during this time, all serving as members of Douglas Bader's No.242 Squadron. Of the three only

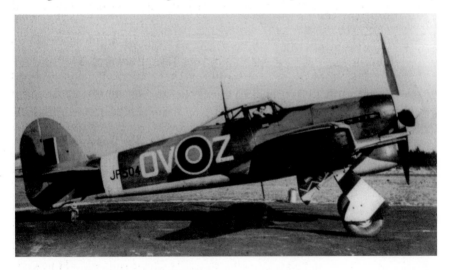

TYPHOON
In September 1941 56 Squadron received its first Typhoons. These were large and heavily armed with 12 .303 machineguns. Initially they were beset with structural problems and a number were lost, together with their pilots.

Sub/Lt R E (Jimmy) Gardener RNVR survived the War. Following his service with No.242 and a stint with Coastal Command, he returned to the Navy. After an eventful time on aircraft carriers in the Mediterranean he was appointed CO of 736 Squadron flying Seafires at RNAS Yeovilton. On leaving the Navy, in March 1946, he was appointed Chief Flying Instructor for the School of Naval Warfare.

By the end of October the Duxford Wing had really run its course. There were now very few daylight raids although German fighters continued to make sweeps over Southern England. One such occasion was on 5th November when the squadrons were on patrol No.19 Squadron saw ten Bf109s between Dover and Deal. In the ensuing fight Sgt Charnock claimed a certainty and Flight Lieutenant 'Farmer' Lawson claimed a probable.

Later the same day the squadrons were scrambled to intercept a group of 42 enemy aircraft that had crossed the coast at Ramsgate. As they patrolled between Canterbury and Dover, No.310 Squadron's Hurricanes were bounced by some Bf109s. Five Hurricanes were hit. Sergeants Jiroudek and Puda managed to bail out and three others crashed on landing.

Bader's No.242 Squadron also engaged the enemy and two of its Hurricanes were lost. Pilot Officer Norris Hart, one of the Canadian pilots disappeared without trace, presumably crashing into the sea. His name is listed on the Runnymede Memorial. Sub Lieutenant Jimmy Gardner suffered serious damage to his Hurricane, but he managed to crash land at Rochford. However, Pilot Officer Frantisek Hradil of No.310 Squadron was not so lucky and was killed when his Hurricane crashed in flames near Southend Pier.

During that afternoon Flight Lieutenant 'Farmer' Lawson of No.19 Squadron was flying the new cannon-armed Spitfire, R6889. He later reported that when he attacked a Bf109 after only about 20 rounds per gun, it 'literally fell to pieces'.

On 8th November Squadron Leader Lane nearly came to grief. No.19 Squadron were patrolling over Canterbury when a Bf109 dived out of the cloud just in front of them. The Bf109 was hotly pursued by a Hurricane that was firing its guns. One of the Hurricane's bullets hit the engine of Brian Lane's Spitfire completely disabling it. Fortunately he managed to crash-land at Eastchurch.

Another casualty occurred on 15th November after No.19 and No.242 Squadrons had been detailed to patrol a convoy 20 miles east of Harwich. They never found the convoy, but did succeed in shooting down two Bf110s.

When they got back to Fowlmere the weather had closed in and visibility was poor. During his final approach Sergeant Henry Roden struck a tree on the leeward boundary. His Spitfire, P7420 was written off and Sergeant Roden was seriously injured. He died the following day and was later buried near his family home at Linlithgow, West Lothian.

At this time, Britain's night defences were so unsophisticated that the Germans were virtually able to go where they pleased – so long as they could find it. As Henry Roden lay dying in Cambridge, news came through that during the previous night 449 German bombers had flown right across England and dropped 400 tonnes of high explosive on Coventry, devastating the city centre and causing some 1,350 casualties.

As a desperate measure Spitfires and Hurricanes were pressed into service as night fighters, but with no radar or any other means of detecting the enemy it was very much hit and miss – usually miss. Not only were the defenders unable to see the enemy, but they were unable to see each other. The only way to minimise mid-air collisions was to keep strictly to previously agreed altitudes and flight plans. The combined strain of night flying using instruments was obviously considerable.

By now the Battle of Britain was over. A total of 71 RAF squadrons officially took part in the Battle and 1,065 RAF aircraft were lost, including 1,004 fighters. Regrettably, 544 pilots also lost their lives. Eight squadrons operated from Duxford at various times during the Battle and their reported losses were as follows, although it should be noted that not all of these losses were while the squadron was based at Duxford.

No.19 Squadron : 6 pilots killed in action
No.74 Squadron : 12 pilots killed in action
No.242 Squadron : 5 pilots killed in action
No.266 Squadron : 7 pilots killed in action
No.302 Squadron : 6 pilots killed in action
No.310 Squadron : 2 pilots killed in action
No.312 Squadron : 1 pilot killed in action
No.616 Squadron : 6 pilots killed in action

At the end of November No.242 Squadron finally left Duxford and returned to Coltishall, leaving No.19 and No.310 Squadrons to continue with defensive patrols. These included night time patrols by No.19 Squadron from Fowlmere. However, by the end of November the weather was so bad that flying came to a full stop as far as No.19 Squadron was concerned.

On 16th January 1941, King George VI and Queen Elizabeth visited Duxford. The King held an investiture that included a DFC for Sq/Ldr Sasha Hess, the joint CO of No.310 Squadron, in recognition to his squadron's contribution to the Duxford Wing.

Night raids continued. The worst came on the night of 25th February at about 11.00 pm, eight bombs fell on the Duxford flare path, with another high explosive bomb on No.310 Squadron's dispersal. This bomb set fire to a fuel bowser causing the deaths of two of the Czech airmen, with five more injured. The dead airmen were buried in the graveyard of nearby Whittlesford Church, along with a number of other wartime casualties from RAF Duxford, but these two deaths were the only ones that were the result of wartime bombing.

The winter of 1940-1941 proved to be a quiet time after the hectic months of the previous summer and early autumn. During the moonlight period of March a total of 35 German aircraft had been knocked out by a combination of fighters and anti-aircraft guns. Apart from the occasional patrol, for No.310 and No.19 Squadrons there was little action during daylight hours. This was replaced by training. As Brian Lane pointed out in his book, even experienced pilots needed to keep their hands in, with new tactics evolved and night flying training became necessary

Early 1941 was a time of change at RAF Duxford as squadrons were being given new roles and so the station began to be the home of a number of specialist units. No.19 Squadron moved to Fowlmere once again in order to make more room at Duxford for the Air Fighting Development Unit (AFDU) that had originally been set up at Northolt to evaluate new aircraft and systems. Arriving alongside this was the Air Gun Mounting Unit, which concentrated on armament and had already carried out work to remedy the problems with the wing-mounted cannons on No.19 Squadron's Mk IB Spitfires. Both of these units moved in and by the spring of 1941 had settled down to routine work. They were later joined by the Naval Air Fighting Development Unit (NAFDU), 787 Squadron of the Fleet Air Arm, which flew shipboard types such as the Fulmer and Martlet.

In late June 1941, No.310 Squadron moved out to RAF Martlesham Heath and was replaced by No.56 (Punjab) Squadron, also flying Hurricanes. No.56 had been heavily engaged in the Battle of Britain, mainly when stationed at North Weald. This squadron had been chosen to trial the new Hawker Typhoon once it became available later in the year.

On 15th June Brian Lane bade farewell to No.19 Squadron and Duxford when he was posted to 12 Group HQ for staff duties. His replacement was Sq/Ldr Roy Dutton who was not at Duxford for very long because on 16th August No.19 Squadron also said a final goodbye when it moved to RAF Matlask. No.133 Squadron, another Hurricane squadron, arrived at Duxford in August before moving to Fowlmere in October.

No.19 was the last of Duxford's Battle of Britain squadrons to leave. By this point, the Squadron had been associated with RAF Duxford and its satellite at Fowlmere for 18 years since it was reformed on 1st April 1923. Especially in recent times it had moved backwards and forwards between Duxford and Fowlmere, where it had officially been based since February.

No.19 Squadron was replaced the same day by No.601 (City of London) Squadron, which arrived to train on the new and unusual Bell Airacobra. This was the only RAF squadron to be equipped with this rare American fighter. The aircraft was essentially designed around a large T-9 cannon that fired through the centre of the propeller hub, which necessitated mounting the Allison engine behind the pilot with the prop shaft running between the pilot's legs. The Airacobra's tricycle undercarriage was a rarity at the time. The aircraft was fast and heavily armed, but not at all easy to fly. And pilots also had to wrestle with almost incessant engine problems.

No.601 was the first of Trenchard's auxiliary squadrons that were made up of amateur pilots who could be swiftly mobilised on the outbreak of war. It was created by Lord Grosvenor and was originally known as the Millionaire's Squadron because according to legend Grosvenor required members to belong to the gentleman's club Whites. It was said that recruitment involved trial by alcohol because Grosvenor only wanted to recruit gentlemen. His theory being that a candidate would still behave like a gentleman when drunk only if he were a real gentleman.

By the summer of 1941 nearly all of the squadron's original members were either dead or had been posted elsewhere. Coincidentally, exactly a week before No.601's arrival at Duxford Douglas Bader flew his last operational sortie of the War. For some time he had been leading the Tangmere Wing, made up of No.616, No.610 and No.41 Squadrons. On 22nd June his aircraft wsa brought down over France and he was taken prisoner by the Germans. .

In September 1941, 1426 (Enemy Aircraft) Flight was formed at Duxford. This was a unit of the AFDU and had something of a celebrity status because it flew captured enemy aircraft for demonstration and evaluation purposes.

The collection included two Junkers Ju88s, a Heinkel He 111, a Messerschmitt Bf109 and a Messerschmitt Bf110. The following year a captured Focke Wulf Fw190 was also added to the collection. The aircraft made frequent flights and although RAF roundels were prominently displayed on them, other RAF aircraft always escorted them.

Also in September 1941, No.56 Squadron's new Hawker Typhoons arrived. The squadron was to trial this new aircraft in operational conditions before it was ready for combat in general service. Like the Hurricane it had been designed by Sydney Camm and had first flown in February 1940. It was large for a fighter, was powered by a Napier Sabre engine and came heavily armed with twelve .303 machineguns.

Problems with the aircraft soon became apparent. Structural weakness caused a number of aircraft to be lost when their tail units fell off; the undercarriages also had a tenancy to collapse; all-round visibility was poor and the cockpit leaked carbon monoxide, causing one pilot to die as a result of carbon monoxide poisoning. The engine was also temperamental and

DIEPPE RETURN
On 19th August 1943 three Duxford Typhoon squadrons gave support to the ill-fated Dieppe Landings, code named Operation Jubilee. Of the 6,086 troops who made it ashore, 3,623 were killed, wounded or captured. Those left made a tactical withdrawal.

DE HAVILLAND MOSQUITO

The De Havilland Mosquito was of an all–wood construction that relied on a new type of synthetic glue called Redux that was very effective for bonding wood to wood, wood to metal, and metal to metal. Coincidentally the adhesive was made at a factory very close to RAF Duxford.

prone to cutting out at high speeds. On top of all this, the aircraft was very heavy and difficult to control, resulting in an unusually high number of training accidents.

On 9th October No.601 Squadron took its Airacobras on a raid on the French coast, but the aircraft were not considered to be a success so by December the squadron began to convert to Spitfires. The following month the squadron left Duxford for the Yorkshire station of RAF Acaster Malbis.

Another interesting Duxford resident at this time was the No.74 (Signals) Wing. This was based on the south side of the airfield and was involved in coastal radar calibration work. The wing used a variety of aircraft including Blenheim IVs, Hornet Moths and the rather unusual Cierva autogyro.

By January 1942, in addition its collection of enemy aircraft, the AFDU had gathered an interesting collection of other aircraft. The first and highly secret De Havilland Mosquito was undergoing trials there. The findings raised a few eyebrows when it was declared that the Mosquito was actually faster than the Spitfire.

Also on test during the spring was the new North American Mustang Mk I with an Allison engine. The Air Ministry had been impressed by this new fighter and had placed an immediate order, but it was soon found that although it was very capable at low altitudes, above 15,000 feet the Mustang's performance was inadequate. These problems were overcome when Rolls Royce engineers re-engined it with one of their Merlins.

The Merlin-engined Mustang went on to become one of the most successful fighters with both the RAF and the USAAF. Known as the P-47 by the Americans, 15,683 were eventually built – more than any other American fighter. One of the ironies is that its co-designer, Edgar Schmued, had previously worked for Fokker and Messerschmitt.

Other aircraft being trialed at AFDU at Duxford were the North American Mitchell, the Martin Marauder, the Lockheed Ventura and several Hurricanes that had been modified for a bombing role. There was also a Vickers Wellington with a huge 40 mm cannon in its tail.

In January 1942, No.266 (Rhodesia) Squadron had arrived at Duxford with the intention of re-equipping with Typhoons. However, since the various problems had delayed production the squadron kept its Spitfire MkVBs.

March saw the arrival of No.609 (West Riding) Squadron when it joined No.56 and 266 Squadrons with the intention of establishing a Typhoon Wing. 609 Squadron was one of the 'Territorial' Royal Auxiliary Air Force squadrons and during the Battle of Britain had been based at Middle Wallop as part of 10 Group. During August 1940 the squadron destroyed 46 enemy aircraft and on 21st October 1940 became the first squadron to achieve 100 confirmed enemy aircraft kills. By then very few of the original pre-war pilots were still alive but one, Pilot Officer David Moore Crook, did survive and after destroying six of the enemy was awarded a DFC. The Spitfire that he often flew is now on display in the Imperial War Museum in London. Sadly David Crook did not survive the War. On 18th December 1944 while training for high-level photographic reconnaissance his Spitfire XI dived into the sea off Aberdeen from a height of 22,000 feet. He is also commemorated on the Runnymede Memorial.

Another noted member of No.609 Squadron, although he did not actually serve at Duxford, was Berlin-born Klaus Hugo Adam. Klaus escaped to

England from Nazi Germany in 1934 when he was 12 years old. On leaving school he trained as an architect before joining the RAF as a fighter pilot in 1941and becoming a member of No.609 Squadron in October 1943 flying Typhoons. By then he had changed his name to Kenneth.

After the war he became a highly regarded film set designer, being nominated for five Oscars and winning two. In 1999 he designed the interior of the Berlin Millennium Exhibition Pavilion and in 2003 received a knighthood for services to the film industry and Anglo-German relations.

By April 1942 the Typhoon Wing had become a reality and was commanded by Wing Commander Denys Gillam. The Typhoon's problems seemed to be over and on 9th June the Wing flew in a demonstration for the Duke of Kent. The following day it gave a demonstration for the Chiefs of Fighter Command and 12 Group.

In May 1942 an Avro Lancaster was evaluated at Duxford. Bomber Command was anxious to know how to develop evasive tactics for heavy bombers, due to the heavy losses that had been inflicted during their daylight raids.

On 20th June the Typhoon Wing's undertook its first operational mission was when it made an offensive sweep over Northern France. On this occasion the Station Commander, Group Captain John Grandy, later to be Marshall of the Royal Air Force Sir John Grandy, took part.

The same month RAF Fowlmere and RAF Duxford became involved in an interesting and unusual project. Noël Coward had written, was co-directing and starring in the film In Which we Serve, which was based on the sinking of Louis Mountbatten's ship, HMS Kelly. In view of the immense propaganda value of the film its makers were granted extensive and unprecedented co-operation by the military authorities.

Although all the interior scenes were filmed at Denham Film Studios and the scenes of the survivors on their life raft were filmed in the Denham Film Studio tank, all of the scenes where the ship was being attacked by enemy bombers were filmed at RAF Fowlmere. A mock-up of the destroyer's superstructure was built on a corner of the airfield and the Junkers Ju88 from Duxford's 1426 Enemy Aircraft Flight was then filmed making the attack.

The completed film was nominated in the 1943 Academy Awards for Best Picture and Best Original Screenplay and Noël Coward was presented with an Academy Honorary Award for "his outstanding production achievement."

On 12th August 1942 1st Lt J A Glenn of the 1st Fighter Group, USAAF became the first American pilot to fly into Duxford when he arrived from Gloxhill in a Lockheed P-38 Lightning that was on tactical trials. This turned out to be the shape of things to come.

On 19th August came Operation Jubilee. This was the code name given to the ill-fated Dieppe Landing Operation. The three Typhoon squadrons joined four Spitfire IX and 42 Spitfire V and VI squadrons, plus eight squadrons of Hurricane fighter-bombers, four squadrons of reconnaissance Mustangs, seven squadrons of Blenheim and Boston light bombers, a squadron of Beaufighters and four squadrons of US B-17s to provide support for the troops as they landed.

A force of this size had not been brought together for one operation since the Battle of Britain two years previously. In fact it was far greater than the one Dowding had. Air Vice-Marshal Trafford Leigh-Mallory had responsibility for providing air cover and his idea was to lure the Luftwaffe into battle, when the RAF would be ready for them. The role of the Spitfires in this operation was to provide air support for the landings and to be prepared to jump on any of the enemy that tried to interfere.

In theory this was a fine idea, but in practice it was doomed. Since the Spitfires were operating 60 miles from the English coast they were often more than 100 miles from base so could not patrol for more than about 30 minutes.

NOEL COWARD

June 1942 saw RAF Fowlmere transformed for Noel Coward's film *In Which We Serve*. This was based on the story of the sinking of HMS Kelly, captained by Coward's friend Lord Louis Mountbatten. While all the interiors were shot at Denham Film Studios, all the exteriors were filmed at Fowlmere using specially constructed sets and captured German aircraft.

FW190

The FW 190 was very fast and very hard to catch. The only RAF aircraft that were a real match for the FW 190s were the new Typhoons. They were used for the first time during Operation Jubilee and in spite of some structural problems, they were able to prove their value.

This needed very complicated planning to achieve constant cover for the landing ships below. Meanwhile the Luftwaffe's aircraft were operating close to their bases, which meant that they stay in the combat area for longer because they were able to refuel swiftly when necessary.

As if this wasn't enough, the RAF had believed that it would have numerical superiority, but early on it became very clear that in reality the two sides were numerically very evenly matched. Although this turned out to be a one-sided fight because most of the German Fighters were Fw190s that were far superior to the ageing Spitfire V and VIs.

The Spitfires were the aircraft that were supposed to be protecting the ships but they were simply shot out of the sky. The landings began at around 5.00 am and by 10.00 am no ship was safe from attack, with nearly all suffering at least some damage.

By now Johnnie Johnson was commanding No.610 Squadron and for this mission was part of 12 Group Wing led by Jamie Jamieson. Jamieson had been one of only a handful of survivors from the sinking of HMS Glorious in the Arctic Ocean in 1940 while he was a Flight Lieutenant with No.46 Squadron.

Jameson managed to survive by climbing on to a Carley float with Squadron Leader Cross and 61 seamen. Several days later they were picked up by a passing fishing vessel, by which time 25 of the seamen had died from exposure and exhaustion.

Jamie Jamieson graphically illustrated what it was like to me a member of a Spitfire Wing at Dieppe:

On arrival over Dieppe the Wing was immediately bounced by 100 FW190s and a few Bf109s. My section was attacked at least twenty times in as many minutes. After about ten minutes a further fifty FW190s were seen coming from the east to reinforce the first bunch.

At a planning conference before the raid Group Captain Harry Broadhurst, now Deputy Senior Air Staff Officer at 11 Group had voiced his opinion that Wings of three squadrons were too cumbersome for such an operation. He was overruled by Leigh-Mallory. Broadhurst was given permission to fly on the raid and borrowed a Spitfire from Hornchurch to go and see for himself.

He immediately noticed that once they reached the French coast the higher and faster Fw190s bounced the RAF Wings, causing them to split up and never reform. He realised that the RAF aircraft would be far better flying in pairs and fours where they could dive out of the sun and catch the Fw190s as they started their dives on the ships below. When he returned he telephoned Leigh-Mallory to tell him so.

Leigh-Mallory was a passionate supporter of Big Wings and what Broadhurst had to say was nothing short of heresy. Broadhurst's advice was initially refused, but Leigh-Mallory respected Broadhurst and the operational instructions were later changed. Leigh-Mallory was fully aware that Broadhurst was also a supporter of the Big Wing principle, but he appreciated the need for flexibility and the fact that Big Wings weren't the answer to every situation.

The three Typhoon squadrons from Duxford acquitted themselves rather well and it was during this operation that their existence was officially acknowledged for the first time. However, it was clear that the earlier problems with this aircraft had still not been fully overcome because when a group of Typhoons dived out of the sun and bounced a formation of Fw190s south of Le Treport, although they damaged three of the German fighters, two of the Typhoons were lost when they were unable to pull out of their dives due to structural failures in their tail assemblies.

In the event, none of the major objectives of Operation Jubilee was accomplished, although it was later acknowledged to have been an excellent rehearsal for how not to conduct the D-Day landings. In reality a total of 3,623 of the 6,086 troops (almost 60%) who made it ashore were killed, wounded, or captured. A Royal Naval officer described it as a "sea version of the Charge of the Light Brigade."

The Royal Navy lost 33 landing craft and one destroyer, and the RAF lost 96 aircraft, including 59 Spitfires. Leigh-Mallory actually hailed it as a great victory for his fighter squadrons claiming 271 enemy aircraft destroyed. As usual this was way above the true figure. German records show an actual loss of 48 aircraft including those destroyed on the ground. Although the RAF had given a good account of itself and had achieved part of its aim in drawing the Luftwaffe into battle, it had suffered losses and had certainly not made the significant inroads on the Luftwaffe, which had been Leigh-Mallory's prime intention.

The Typhoons had shown that they were capable of providing a big punch in combat conditions, despite unreliability. Another of the problems that rapidly manifested itself was that in appearance the Typhoons bore a very striking resemblance to the Fw190s, making them very likely to become victims of friendly fire. To counteract the continual risk of mistaken identity various colour configurations were successively painted on the wings and fuselages of the Typhoons.

By the late summer of 1942 the commanders of the three Typhoon squadrons were accepting that the Wing had not proved to be the success that was hoped for. Given the speed and firepower of the aircraft, their proposal was that the Typhoon squadrons could be better and more effectively used by operating independently at airfields closer to the coast. This judgement was very much in line with what Broadhurst had been saying over Dieppe. This became accepted and by the autumn the three squadrons moved away from Duxford to more forward bases where they were better able to counter the Luftwaffe's high-speed low-level fighter-bomber attacks.

On 1st September 1942 a further Typhoon squadron was formed at Duxford. This was No.181 Squadron, commanded by Sq/Ldr D Crowley Milling, who two years before had been a young Pilot Officer in Douglas

Bader's No.242 Squadron. By December the squadron had completed its training and it left for RAF Snailwell.

Even with its troubled beginnings, and although it continued to be mistaken for the Focke Wulf Fw190, the Typhoon went on to become one of World War II's most successful ground attack aircraft. In fact the entire project was probably only saved from cancellation by the realisation that the Typhoon was the only RAF aircraft capable of catching the Fw190 at low level.

Throughout 1942 the effects of the US entry into the War were gradually making themselves felt. The rapid expansion of the USAAF had brought a pressing need for airfield space and by September it had been decided that Duxford was to be one of the RAF bases handed over to the USAAF 8th Air Force. This move was somewhat overshadowed in November by Operation Torch, when the Allies invaded French North Africa, at that time controlled by the Vichy French.

For this operation the Americans established the 12th Air Force under the command of Major General James Doolittle. Special authority was granted to the Americans to allow them to use Duxford as part of the operation's preparation. On 1st October a new US Fighter Group, the 350th Fighter Group was formed under the command of Major R F Klocko and this arrived at Duxford by the end of the month.

CROWLING-MILLING
Sq Ldr D Crowley-Milling took command of a new Typhoon squadron, Number 181, at Duxford on 1st September 1942. Two years before he had been a Pilot Officer in Douglas Bader's 242 Squadron. After three months training at Duxford the squadron left for RAF Snailwell.

This Fighter Group had three squadrons, the 345th, 346th and 347th, comprising mostly of American pilots who had already been serving with RAF or Royal Canadian Air Force units in Britain. Since there was still a considerable amount of RAF activity at Duxford, initially only the Group HQ and the 345th Squadron could be accommodated there, with the 346th being detached to Coltishall and the 347th to Snailwell.

By January 1943 all three squadrons were at Duxford with Bell Airacobras, the P-400 that the RAF had rejected a few months earlier. This was only to be a temporary stay because in late January and early February the whole Group, with its 61 tan-painted aircraft, left Duxford for Oujda in French Morocco to join the US 12th Air Force as part of Operation Torch.

The last RAF unit to squeeze into Duxford before the formal American takeover was No.169 Squadron that arrived from Clifton for a short stay in December. This squadron was equipped with North American Mustangs that they used in a programme of shipping reconnaissance and ground-attack missions.

The early months of 1943 saw a general exodus of the RAF from Duxford bringing a short period of calm as the Americans prepared to take complete control. The AFDU, which had been trying out American P-38 Lightnings and P-47 Thunderbolts, together with the NAFDU both moved to RAF Wittering and 1426 Flight with its captured enemy aircraft moved to Wittering's satellite station at RAF Collyweston. No.74 (Signals) Wing became No. 1448 (Radar Calibration) Flight when it moved to RAF Halton and 169 Squadron with its Mustangs went to RAF Barford St John in Oxfordshire.

By mid-March flying at RAF Duxford was at a minimum and the stage was now set for the next chapter in the station's history.

The American Intervention

B etween 1943 and 1945 RAF Duxford was one of many RAF stations that were loaned to the United States Army Air Force (USAAF). When the United States entered the War it was far from being unprepared. In 1938 the worsening political state of Europe had led President Roosevelt to call for a strengthening of the country's air defence. By May 1941, while the US was still neutral, a special US Army Observer

P-47 THUNDERBOLT
The P-47s were the heaviest single seater fighters of World War II. They were rugged and popular with pilots, being well able to hold their own with Bf 109s and FW 190s. Their only drawbacks were their lack of range and the fact that were often confused with FW190s.

Group began to reconnoitre areas regarded as potential sites for USAAF installations in Britain.

On 7th December 1941 the Japanese attacked Pearl Harbor and four days later Germany declared war on the US. Less than three weeks later Churchill and Roosevelt met in Washington DC as war leaders for the first time. The decisions made at this meeting had a direct influence on the establishment of the US Eighth Air Force in the UK.

The USAAF formed sixteen separate air forces during World War II and the Eighth Air Force was the largest of them all – in due course it became known as the 'Mighty Eighth'. It eventually had twice the number of heavy bomber squadrons as RAF Bomber Command. Fighter support was an essential element of the US strategic plan and there were 20 Fighter Groups in addition to the 47 Bomber Groups.

Given the vast number of aircraft an enormous number of airfields were needed. Ultimately 92 airfields were used by the Eighth, mostly in Eastern England. While some were former RAF stations, many others were new-builds. At its peak in 1942, a third of the UK construction industry was engaged in building airfields, with a new airfield being completed every two to three weeks.

RAF Duxford was one of the airfields to be handed over to the USAAF and on 24th March 1943 a convoy of trucks arrived carrying the advance party of the 78th Fighter Group of the United States Army Air Force. From then a process began that was to transform RAF Duxford into part of Little America. The Red Cross replaced the NAAFI and the curved roofed Nissan Huts, so common on all military bases, became known as Quonsets. The Aeroclub, the Officers' Club, the Sergeants' Club and Duffy's Tavern were all established. The Station Dances were to become legendary and attracted girls from a wide area.

While the RAF's practice had always been to name a station after the nearest village or parish in which it was situated, the American practice was to give each one a number and Duxford was to become Station 357. The 78th Fighter Group had been formed in May 1942 and had trained on P-38 Lightnings in California. On 1st December 1943 the Group moved to RAF Goxhill in Lincolnshire to familiarise themselves with the kind of conditions likely to be experienced once they became operational in East Anglia.

By Christmas most of the tools and equipment had arrived together with a few of their aircraft. For many American airmen Gloxhill was remembered

US B-17 OVER NURNBERG

It was initially thought that large groups of heavily armed bombers in tight formations would be able to defend themselves during daylight raids. This proved to be incorrect and casualty rates were very high. Initially there were no fighters with sufficient range to accompany the bombers on raids deep into Germany.

for the mud and the tents that housed the stores and the latrines, but many others remembered the very warm welcome that they found in the homes of local people during their first Christmas away from home.

In January 1943, as the Group was building up to operational strength with its P-38s, a handful of P-47C Thunderbolts arrived at Goxhill. These were new aircraft and the pilots had a chance to try them out, although few had ever considered flying anything other than a P-38 when it came to combat. *Operation Torch* changed all that. The invasion of French North Africa created a sudden demand for pilots and aircraft to support the 12th Air Force.

As a resuilt, the 78th Group lost all of its P–38s and all but 15 of its experienced pilots.

As result it was decided that the 78th Group would be re-equipped with P–47C Thunderbolts and new pilots were rushed to Goxhill to begin a hurried training period. This was completed in almost record time and under the command of Lt Col Arman Peterson, the move to Duxford came on 1st April. This was a considerable logistical exercise since it involved transporting some 1,700 personnel in addition to the Group's 75 Republic P–47C Thunderbolts, not to mention all the associated equipment and spares.

Having moved into Duxford, the Group began working up its three squadrons, the 82nd, 83rd and 84th to operational status. By the end of their first week, on Thursday 8th April, twelve Duxford aircraft were able to join with a similar number of 4th Group aircraft based at Debden in flying an uneventful sweep.

The 78th's first true mission took place on 13th April when Lt Col Peterson led the 12 Thunderbolts of 83rd Squadron in a joint mission with two squadrons of Debden aircraft in a sweep over North East France. Flying at 30,000 feet they penetrated as far as the Luftwaffe base at St Omer, but saw no sign of either enemy aircraft or flak.

On the way back, due to engine failure Lt Col Joseph L Dickman was forced to bail out over the sea northeast of Calais. He was picked up by an RAF air-sea rescue launch and was awarded the Group's first Purple Heart. Less than 4½ hours after he had landed, Lt Col Peterson returned to the St Omer area, this time with 12 aircraft from the 82nd Squadron at Duxford, plus a squadron from 4th Group at Debden and another from 56th Group based at Horsham St Faiths. Again, nothing was sighted.

It was two days later on 15th April that the first enemy aircraft were sighted. The 84th sent up 12 aircraft and the 82nd and 83rd put up six each to form a second squadron. They were joined by a squadron from Debden and while patrolling over Belgium they spotted some enemy planes over an airfield, but the enemy disappeared into cloud before they could be engaged.

The 78th struck out by itself for the first time on 17th April when Lt Col Peterson led two squadrons of 16 aircraft each on two missions, but both proved uneventful and the 78th soon settled into a familiar pattern of operations.

On 20th May came something of a turning point. Previously the 78th had been involved in patrols as a fighter unit, but this time they were acting as support for bombers that were attacking Antwerp. Peterson had just been promoted to full colonel and he was leading a group of three squadrons with 16 aircraft in each when they encountered a group of more than 20 Fw190s and Bf109s.

This was a day of action. Maj J Stone, CO of 83rd Squadron and Capt Robert Adamina both shot down Fw190s but three pilots, Capt Adamina, F/O S R Martinek and Capt McTaggart were lost, although all three survived. Capt Adamina managed to land his Thunderbolt on the sea and is believed to be the first and only pilot to have done this successfully. F/O Samuel Martinek was captured and spent the rest of the War as a POW, but Capt Elmer McTaggart managed to evade capture and eventually made it across the Pyrenees and into Spain, losing 25 pounds in weight on the journey.

At the end of the day, although three aircraft and three pilots were lost, as opposed to only two of the enemy, the success of the Thunderbolts in protecting the bombers strengthened the belief among senior officers that daylight bomber raids, supported by a strong fighter escort, was the way forward.

On 26th May, King George VI and Queen Elizabeth paid a visit to Duxford to officially welcome the 78th Fighter Group to the station, or 'field' as it was now known. By then the transition from being an RAF 'station' to a USAAF 'field' was almost complete and on 15th June 1943 Wg/Cdr Matthews the RAF Station Commander formally handed over command to Col Peterson.

All through May and June operations had been fairly routine, with very little action and few losses. The P-47D had now been introduced into service and this was found to be an improvement on the earlier P-47C version.

By mid-summer of 1943 the 78th Fighter Group had begun to establish a high reputation for itself. It was certainly the most successful of the three Fighter Groups, the other two being at Debden and Horsham St Faiths. Morale was high and it was given an additional boost by visits from well-known stars of cinema and radio such as Bing Crosby, Bob Hope, James Cagney and Frances Langford.

Bob Hope had begun his regular tours to entertain US forces in 1941 and these were to continue for the next 50 years. During this time he travelled millions of miles. Frances Langford was often part of the company and there is a story that on one occasion she caused uproar because against all regulations she hitched a ride in a P-38. Unfortunately the plane got called into action in the middle of the flight, causing a number of red faces.

The 78th now had its own Dance Band, the Duxford Thunderbolts. As well as playing at station dances, it appeared at venues in Cambridge and London and at other US bases. Radio Shows also came from the base and some were relayed to the US.

On Thursday 1st July Duxford received a serious blow when it lost its CO, the highly respected and well-liked Col Arman (Pete) Peterson. The Group was in a fierce action that resulted in the destruction of four Fw190s, plus a probable and damage to five others. The only American loss was Peterson who had been CO of the Group since its formation in May the previous year. It seems that he bailed out over Southern Holland but as he descended, a German soldier shot his parachute apart and he fell to the ground. He was initially buried in the cemetery in the village of Goedereede, but his body was later re-buried in the family plot in Thatcher Cemetery, Arizona.

Peterson was 28 years old and an enormously popular leader and his loss was felt very deeply by everyone at Duxford. Morale sagged. It was the Saturday of Holiday Weekend when Bob Hope visited the base with Frances Langford. Even Hope admitted that he had trouble getting laughs out of his audience. There was not much 4th July holiday spirit on the following day either. A midday mission was followed by an outdoor supper on the athletic field, but it was all a bit flat.

The new CO arrived on 12th July. He was Lt Col Melvin McNickle, who had previously served at Duxford when he was USAAF liaison officer with the RAF's No.601 Squadron while they were evaluating the Bell Airacobras in the autumn of 1941. Two days later there was celebration when a Duxford pilot was awarded a Distinguished Service Cross, which is the second highest US award for valour. 2nd Lt A V DeGenaro of the 82nd had been escorting a bomber force that attacked an airfield at Amiens. After destroying two Fw190s and damaging another, Lt DeGenaro received severe injuries in both hands, his right knee and both ankles resulting in him having to fly his Thunderbolt using his forearms.

His aircraft's instruments had been shot away, its right wing was badly shot up and its tail surfaces were damaged. Three Fw190s were following De Genaro but he managed to evade them by ducking into some low clouds. Eventually he reached the English coast, intending to make a crash landing, but soon realised that he had unfastened his seat belt and because of his injuries he was not able to do it up again. His only option was to bail out but if he did so his aircraft was almost certain to crash on the coastal town below. This led him to turn his aircraft seawards once more and he eventually bailed out over the Channel in full view of a fishing boat that then rescued him.

30th July was another eventful day. It was the first occasion that the fighters carried drop tanks, which enabled them to fly right into Germany. The pilots claimed 16 victories, seven Bf109s and nine Fw190s, and thus became the first American unit to achieve victories that ran into double figures in a single mission.

During that mission Capt Charles London of the 83rd shot down a Bf109 and a Fw190 making him the first American pilot to shoot down five aircraft in the European Theatre. This officially credited him with the title 'ace'. Maj Eugene Roberts downed two Fw190s and a Bf109, making him the first American in the European theatre to get a 'triple' by destroying three of the enemy in one mission. For fighting off superior enemy forces and for getting his 'triple' he was awarded the Group's second Distinguished Service Cross.

BING CROSBY

Entertainment was very important and Duxford had excellent theatre facilities that were very popular with visiting stars. These shows were a great morale booster and Bing Crosby was always a welcome attraction.

Lt Quince Brown had engine trouble and lost altitude, but took the opportunity while hedge-hopping to shoot up a freight locomotive and a gun battery to the west of Rotterdam, making it the first recorded incident of ground strafing by an Eighth Air Force pilot.

Two American pilots were lost that day. One managed to evade capture, but the other, Lt Col Melvin McNickle who had been CO for just under than a month, was shot down and became a prisoner of war. His replacement as Station CO was Lt Col James Stone, who was promoted from being CO of the 83rd Squadron. Lt Col Stone had been with the 78th since its formation and had the distinction of achieving its first victory.

On 4th September General Hap Arnold, commander-in-chief of the USAAF, visited Duxford. He was shown around, watched a display of the latest British and American fighter aircraft and gave a lecture on the history and future role of the American Air Force.

The remainder of the year was taken up with fairly routine escort missions and sweeps. These were quite exhausting with many sorties lasting for more than five hours. Naturally concentration could never be allowed to flag because at any moment there could be an attack by German fighters.

Unlike many other USAAF bases, Duxford was fairly comfortable. Elsewhere while many airbase personnel had to make do with hastily erected Nissen or Quonset huts, or even tents, most Duxford personnel had centrally heated barracks with electric light and tiled shower rooms. It was widely regarded as being 'one of the finest and most comfortable of any Army Air Force station overseas.'

There was an Officers' Club, a Sergeants' Club and Aeroclub and a 'Tavern'. One of the big hangers had been converted into a theatre for stage shows or for use as a cinema. Facilities were so good with fine dressing rooms and stage, plus the large seating capacity, that many touring shows particularly requested Duxford as one of their venues. There were also all the usual health facilities on base, with doctors, dentists and first aid treatment rooms. Henceforth, the station was known as the 'Duxford Country Club.'

Escort work continued into the New Year, but by January 1944 the 78th was ready to start a new type of mission. This was to be fighter bombing. A problem with fighter aircraft had always been that of range. During the Battle of Britain the abiding fear of the Luftwaffe's Bf109 pilots was that they would run out of fuel and have to ditch in the Channel.

Improvements in drop tank technology meant that the Thunderbolt's range was being increased all the time. This enabled a bomb load to be carried to a target and dropped before indulging in some strafing or air combat on the return journey. This type of low-level attack, often on railways and airfields was designed to soften up the enemy in anticipation of the approaching invasion.

The first fighter-bomber mission of the Group took place on 25th January 1944. The brief was to bomb an airfield in France, but bad weather caused the aircraft to return with their bombs. On the last day of the same month, they undertook a second mission and this time thirty-five 500-pound bombs were dropped on the runways of an airfield at Gilze-Rijen in Holland.

BOB HOPE
Bob Hope began entertaining US forces in 1941 and was to continue to do so for the next 50 years. During World War II he toured tirelessly and visited Duxford a number of times, often with Francis Langford and a full company.

HAP ARNOLD
General Henry "Hap" Arnold was Commanding General of the US Army Air Services during World War II. He was an advocate of technological research and development and went on to see the development of the intercontinental bomber, the jet fighter, the extensive use of radar, global airlift and atomic warfare.

In the first week of February the first organised strafing attacks took place. Lt J W Wilkinson of the 82nd and Lt P E Pompetti of the 84th each led a flight that damaged six aircraft on the ground and two Fw190s in the air, together with three freight locomotives and a tugboat. Three airfields were also strafed.

Although the pilots found this exhilarating work, it was highly dangerous, flying at 450 miles per hour at an altitude of less than 100 feet, meant there was a risk of flying into a tall structure, and anti-aircraft fire was dangerously effective. In many ways the Thunderbolts were ideal for this kind of work because in battle they could take an enormous amount of punishment and still get home.

It is worth mentioning that the RAF and the USAAF had very different views with respect to bombing. Early in the War the RAF had tried daylight bombing but high casualty rates had caused them to switch to night time bombing. Since accurate aiming was not easy at night, the RAF favoured what was known as 'area bombing'.

On the other hand the USAAF firmly believed in daylight attacks, using heavily armed bombers, with supporting fighter escorts. They also believed in attacking specific industrial targets, which they felt could be done more successfully in daylight.

Later in February the 78th reverted to escort duty. A 'Blitz Week' had been planned that was aimed at ball bearing factories and aircraft-production centres thus hindering production of the expanding German fighter force. It was considered necessary to allow the allied bomber forces to pursue their strategic bombing programme without excessive losses in order to gain air supremacy for the coming invasion. This was a massive effort involving the 8th and 9th Air Forces in England and the 15th Air Force in Italy. Duxford contributed 10% of the fighters during 'Blitz Week' and claimed 16 victories for the loss of one pilot.

On 6th March the USAAF launched its large-scale raid on Berlin. This involved 702 heavy bombers and a fighter escort of 644 aircraft from both the 8th and 9th Air Forces. Duxford provided the escort for the 1st Bomb Division's B-17 Flying Fortresses. The target was the VKF ball bearing factory at Erkner, south east of Berlin.

The Luftwaffe and the ground defences put up a tremendous fight both on the outward and return journeys. Casualties were enormous, with 69 heavy bombers lost and eleven fighters. The total loss of aircraft and aircrews on this raid was said to have been the largest suffered by the 8th Air Force during the entire air campaign. The 78th lost two pilots, Flying Officer E Downey and 2nd Lieutenant G Turley.

Although Duxford was now a USAAF base, its former satellite at Fowlmere had remained in RAF hands being used by a number of units for short-term attachments. This was to change from April 1944 RAF Fowlmere was also destined to transfer to American use. Immediately prior to this takeover Fowlmere played a key part in Operation Spartan, which was a major exercise in D-Day preparation involving the Spitfire IXs of No.411 Squadron of the Royal Canadian Air Force.

RAF Fowlmere became Station 378 of the USAAF on 5th April. It became the home of the 503rd, 504th and 505th Squadrons of the 339th Fighter Group and was operational from 30th April 1944 to 21st June 1945.

The 339th Fighter Group operated P-51 Mustang fighters and fortunately for these heavier aircraft, the RAF had carried out major improvements to Fowlmere's somewhat basic grass field during the previous summer. Two Pierced Steel Planking (PSP) runways had been laid. One, 1,600 yards long ran from north-east to south-west and the other, 1,400 yards long ran from east to west. Since the latter one ran across the Barley to Fowlmere road, the present B1368, this had been closed. New hangers had been erected plus a number of Nissen huts and accommodation was now much more comfortable than it had previously been. Fowlmere and Duxford were for the first time two completely independent stations in their own right.

Duxford's Thunderbolts operated nearly every day during May 1944, either escorting or strafing. On 19th May, fitted with extra large drop tanks, the 78th supported B-24 Liberators attacking Brunswick. After spending more than four hours in the air the fighter force all returned intact, having shot down ten Bf109s and two Fw190s. This brought the Group's victory total past the 200 mark. It was a fitting climax to the end of Col Stone's service with 78th because on 21st May he handed over command to Lt Col Frederic Gray.

P-47B THUNDERBOLT
The P-47s were initially the mainstay of the Duxford squadrons. They were tough aircraft and could take a lot of punishment, but still make it home to base. Improved drop tanks enabled them to increase their range and by 1944 they were escorting bomber missions deep into Germany.

The beginning of June saw the build up to the allied invasion of Normandy. As tension mounted, Duxford certainly lost its country club atmosphere. Security was tightened, travel was restricted and guns, gas masks and helmets were to be carried at all times.

On the first five days of June the 78th took part in six bomber-support and ground attack missions on coastal defences. On 5th June, after the aircraft returned, all ties between the Station and the outside world were cut. The Royston to Newmarket Road, now the A505 that separates the airfield from the domestic site was closed for the first and only time during the War. Even official traffic was blocked and had to follow diversions.

All telephone communication into and out of the base was blocked with incoming and outgoing mail being frozen. British civilians or American Red Cross workers on or near the field had to remain where they were. Those on post at the time were not allowed to leave and those outside were not permitted to enter. Officers and men crossing the road from the domestic site to the airfield were stopped at the gate and asked their business. If they could not give a satisfactory answer they were not allowed to enter the hanger area. Blackout restrictions were tighter than ever and special wardens patrolled the station to see that these restrictions were enforced.

A special alert flight was put on duty from an hour before sunset to an hour after sunrise. Its task was to be ready to tackle any German air attacks launched in an effort to disrupt the impending invasion. In addition to the regular Military Police (MPs) and anti-aircraft gunners, additional guards were placed around the dispersal areas and a ground defence unit was kept ready in case of an enemy airborne landing.

Inside the security cordon the station was an absolute hive of activity. Personnel who normally never went near an aircraft were given the job of painting black and white invasion stripes on the wings and fuselages of the Thunderbolts, while others suddenly found themselves driving trucks or linking ammunition belts.

Everywhere there was an atmosphere of eager anticipation.

D-Day
and Beyond

During the night of 5th to 6th June sleep was impossible due to the drone of the constant stream of transport aircraft flying overhead and heading south. The transports were packed with paratroopers and many were towing gliders filled with airborne troops and equipment.

On D-Day, 6th June, the 78th had an early start, with the 83rd and 84th squadrons taking off for their first mission at 3.30 am. Their role was to provide cover for the sea-borne landings. In due course the 82nd, which had stayed behind, went out on the second mission as relief for the earlier aircraft. This was the pattern for the rest of the day, with squadrons going on one mission after another, either to bomb specific targets or to strafe transport facilities or targets of opportunity.

The last mission of the day took off at 6.22 pm when the 82nd and 84th Squadrons went out on area support. The 82nd had been told to look for enemy aircraft but could not find them in the dusk, while the 84th damaged a few rail targets. They finally touched down again at Duxford at about 11.00 pm. It had been a long day.

On 7th June the 84th lost two pilots, 1st Lt Harry Just was killed and 1st Lt Hamilton Rice was taken prisoner. For the next two days there was no let-up in the frantic D-Day pace until the weather, which had not been particularly good all week, took a turn for the worse and no missions took off from Duxford on that day.

On 10th June the weather had improved enough to allow four missions to take place. Ground attack was again the objective. On the third mission, just as the Thunderbolts were beginning their bombing run, the Group was attacked by a strong force of Bf109s and Fw190s. That day was one of the costliest that the 78th had experienced in its two years of operation.

Seven pilots were killed, three from the 84th, including the CO Maj Harold Stump, and two each from the 82nd and 83rd. One the fatalities was the result of a mid-air collision, which was always a grave risk during a high-speed dogfight involving a large number of aircraft. Two others, both from the

B-17F, 1942

The B-!7 was a heavily armed bomber, that usually carried a crew of ten. Flying in tight formations it was thought that their massive combined firepower would be sufficient to ensure effective defence against attacking fighters. This proved not to be the case.

84th, were taken prisoner. Although morale did take a bit of a dip, there was little time to grieve as the intensive escort and ground attack work continued. By the end June, 45 missions had been flown for the loss of three more pilots.

In spite of the losses there was a general feeling of a job well done, and soon security began to relax. Travel restrictions were lifted to a distance of 25 miles, so at least the pilots could now enjoy a night out in Cambridge even if they could not get as far as London.

Keeping the aircraft in the air was always a major problem. For this reason the ground engineers of the 84th Service Squadron were presented with a Plaque to acknowledge the fact that during the period from 1st March to 7th June, when the Group had flown approximately 4,400 sorties, the Service Squadron had completed 90% of all repairs in a minimum of time. Sometimes working day and night, and quite often under the most adverse weather conditions.

B-17 DAMAGE
The B-17s were capable of taking a great deal of punishment and there were many instances of seriously damaged aircraft making it back to base, but losses were substantial. On a mission of 700+ bombers it was not unusual for as many as 60 to be lost – this would represent 600 airmen.

In wartime with constant likelihood of being killed in battle, it always seems particularly poignant when death occurs as a result of accident yet this was common. On 1st July 1944 three Thunderbolts collided during take off. Two pilots of the 82nd, 1st Lt Edward Kitley and 2nd Lt Cleon Raese, were killed but the third, 2nd Lt Lester Ford of the 84th, managed to survive both the crash and the war.

There were many training accidents, but the accident that occurred on 19th July 1944 stuck in many memories. The 78th had experienced a good day. Strafing had destroyed 20 enemy aircraft on the ground, which was their largest claim to date. Everyone on the base was feeling good, but in the late afternoon tragedy struck. 1st Lt James D Sasser from the No.412th Bomber Squadron of the 95th Bomber Group flew his B-17 Flying Fortress into Duxford from his base at Horham, 8 miles to the east of Eye in Suffolk. This was technically a training flight, but Lt Sasser had taken the opportunity to visit some friends who were serving with the 84th Squadron at Duxford.

Sasser decided to give some of them a ride. With his own co-pilot and two crewmen, plus Lieutenants John Putnam and Martin Smith of 84th Squadron and eight enlisted men from Duxford, he made a low pass across the control tower intending to pull up over the 84th's hanger.

Unfortunately the aircraft failed to attain sufficient height and clipped the neon blinker light on the top of the hanger. Most of the left wing and the left horizontal stabiliser were promptly sheared off and the bomber rolled over, just missing the officers' barracks but crashing into the main barracks of the 83rd Squadron and part of the main 82nd barracks.

The aircraft had been fully loaded with fuel and there was a massive explosion and fire. All the men on the bomber died, along with one man in the 83rd Squadron's barracks. The Chaplain, Capt William Zink made repeated attempts to reach the man trapped in the barracks, but flames, smoke and falling beams prevented him. He later gave the last rites to the victims and helped medical personnel extricate the bodies from the wreckage. He was subsequently presented with the Soldiers Medal for his actions and was to be the first 8th Air Force chaplain to receive this award. Most of the 83rd's barracks was destroyed. A small mercy is that it occurred when most men were on duty, otherwise loss of life would have been considerably higher.

1st Lieutenant Sasser and 1st Lieutenant Smith are both buried at the US Military Cemetery and Memorial at Madingley, about three miles to the west of Cambridge. It is sited on 30.5 acres of land that was donated by Cambridge

University located on the side of a north-facing hill looking roughly in the direction of where most of the American airbases were sited. The cemetery contains the remains of 3,812 personnel, including five nurses who were killed in road traffic accidents during nights out with pilots who were driving their jeeps on the wrong side of the road. Thirteen of the graves belong to 78th Group pilots who served at Duxford. There is also a Wall of the Missing, giving the names of 5,127 personnel who have no known grave.

One of the 78th Group graves belongs to 31-year-old Capt James Wilkinson of the 82nd. He also died as the result of an accident when his Thunderbolt hit a Welsh mountain while he was practicing strafing techniques two days before D-Day. Sadly this highly respected airman had only recently returned to service after breaking his back in a flying accident the previous year.

A few weeks after his death at a special ceremony, his English widow, Mrs J W Wilkinson, was presented with the Distinguished Service Cross and Silver Star. These her husband had earned on two separate occasions on 19th May 1944, when he had single-handedly fought off and broken up entire squadrons of enemy planes that were attacking US bombers.

To compound the tragedy of Capt Wilkinson's death, a month or two after the presentation of his awards, his widow was found dead in London with a photograph of her late husband lying beside her.

Throughout the summer the 78th continued to achieve victories and then on 28th August the 82nd scored a notable achievement. For a while the allied bomber streams had been plagued by the revolutionary new Luftwaffe fighter, the Messershmitt Me262 Swallow. This was a jet fighter that was faster and better armed than its Allied counterparts. Following its introduction into service in April 1944 its pilots had claimed over 500 victories.

It was so fast that it was rarely ever seen, but on 28th August Maj Joseph Myers and his wingman Lt Manford O'Croy, both of the 82nd Squadron, noticed a 262 flying fast and low to the west of Brussels. After a long chase and a certain amount of tactical manoeuvring, the jet crash-landed in a field. The rest of the squadron then repeatedly strafed it and set it on fire. This was the first time one of these jet aircraft had been shot down.

In September the 78th were fully involved in supporting the Allied airborne landings at Arnhem. Field Marshal Bernard Montgomery had devised a plan to hasten the end of the War by capturing a series of bridges in Holland that would effectively open up a back door into Germany's industrial heartland.

It was a bold plan that involved flying 35,000 Allied troops behind enemy lines, either dropping them by parachute or landing them by glider. The airborne troops would then hold the bridges until the Armoured Corps pushed through the German lines to relieve them.

The operation began on 17th September and the Duxford squadrons were heavily involved in supporting the landings at the bridges of Nijmegen and Arnhem. Their role was to divert enemy fire from the incoming gliders and they were so successful that the Group was awarded a Distinguished Unit Citation and their commanding officer, Col Gray was awarded a silver Cross for his outstanding leadership.

Intelligence had indicated that opposition on the ground would be fairly light, but in reality it proved to be intense and as a result the operation did not go according to plan. By 23rd September further supplies were desperately needed and the 78th Fighter Group was in action against the ground defences as Dakota C-47s and Short Stirlings were sent to drop provisions and equipment to the beleaguered troops. As the American fighters circled Arnhem they met a very heavy barrage of both 20 mm and 40 mm light flak.

Two of the fighter squadrons destroyed concealed guns in a church and along nearby hedgerows, the third squadron of Thunderbolts then also destroyed those guns. However, three of the Dakotas had been shot down by some other flak positions. After that, three more formations of Dakotas and Sterlings came in and safely dropped their supplies right in the middle of what had been a very heavily defended area. The Thunderbolts had neutralised the enemy defences and were credited with saving several scores of supply planes from certain destruction.

Unfortunately the gamble to shorten the War did not come off. Late on 26th September the evacuation of the remaining Allied troops began and by early the next morning the remaining 2,398 survivors had been withdrawn, leaving 300 men to surrender to the Germans at first light. Clearly if Duxford's Thunderbolts had not cleared the way for the supply aircraft, the chance of any survivors would have been minimal.

As autumn began to move into winter, the weather in Eastern England deteriorated. Rain became a serious problem. Duxford was still a grass field therefore was prone to becoming very muddy and often flooded after heavy rain. In fact shortly after the 78th Group arrived they had christened Duxford 'The Duck Pond'.

Pieced Steel Planking (PSP) had already been laid at either end of the runway for when the Thunderbolts were preparing to take off and while this was a bonus when the aircraft were stationary, the aircraft still had to take off and land in water. It was therefore decided to lay a PSP runway 3,500 feet long and 350 feet wide. This was done at the beginning of December and for just over a week the 78th Fighter Group moved ten miles down the road to Bassingbourn, the home of the 91st Bomb Group.

To allow flying to continue, ground crews and pilots had to be ferried backwards and forwards each day by road because all briefing and debriefing continued to be done at Duxford.

Escort work on bombing missions was becoming increasingly important for the fighter squadrons. The problem was that even with drop tanks the tough old Thunderbolts did not have the range for these long missions deep into Germany. As a result North American P-51 Mustangs were gradually being introduced into all the 8th Air Force Fighter Groups.

MUSTANG
Duxford lost its Thunderbolts at the end of 1944, to be replaced by P-51 Mustangs. Pilots found the new aircraft cramped and not so rugged, but they had a far superior range and this is what was needed at that stage of the war.

The 78th flew its last Thunderbolt mission on 31st December 1944 when Capt Julius P Maxwell of the 84th, flying the final sortie of his second tour, shot down a Fw190. This was the 400th German aircraft to be credited to the Group.

A good number of the American pilots were unhappy about having to give up their trusty old Thunderbolts. They were concerned that the liquid-cooled Merlin engines made them more vulnerable to flak during low-level strafing missions, while the cockpits were far less roomy. High Command decreed that the longer range of the Mustang was the decisive factor, but dark tales of things going wrong did not inspire confidence. Crashes were common as the pilots got used to the different characteristics of these very different machines and some of these resulted in fatalities.

Lt "Tom" Bendorf of the 84th Squadron had been one of those unhappy about losing his trusty Thunderbolt. Bendorf was only 20 and was the youngest man in his squadron. He had been assigned a brand new Mustang and on 4th January he was to take it for a 'shakedown' flight over the North Sea for an altitude test and gun check.

The aircraft had been technically checked over and Lt Bendorf headed for the coast. After flying around for some time he climbed to 27,000 feet to test his guns at an altitude where the outside temperature would be around minus 40°. There had been previous reports of guns freezing at these extremely low temperatures, but there seemed to be no problem with his guns. He routinely scanned his instruments and saw to his horror that the engine oil pressure that should have been reading between 70 and 80 pounds per square inch was now reading zero.

He was 100 miles from land and he knew that the Mustang's under-fuselage air scoop did not make ditching a viable option. With the engine temperature rising he nursed his stricken aircraft towards the coast, hoping to make an emergency landing. He crossed the coast at 14,000 feet, by which time the engine was overheating to the point of self-destruction. Finally with a terrific crash it stopped completely and spewed oil and coolant all over the windscreen completely cutting off all forward vision and eliminating the option for making a crash landing.

He knew that his only chance now was to jump. He radioed Duxford to tell them what he was about to do, and they replied that he should phone them when he was on the ground and someone would come and fetch him. His next problem was getting out of the aircraft and that proved to be difficult. An altitude of 600 feet was said to be the minimum survival height for bailing out and he was down to 700 feet before he eventually managed to fall free. Apart from minor bruising he landed safely and his aircraft crashed at Monk Soham 5 miles WNW of Framlingham in Suffolk.

In 1989 the remains of his aircraft were excavated and Tom Bendorf flew over from his home in South Dakota to witness the event. The farmer had cleared some of the wreckage out of the ditch, but the engine was still buried. After this had been dug out and pressure washed, the full extent of its catastrophic failure became evident. All twelve connecting rods had been thrown from the crankshaft making fist-sized holes in the engine casing.

The winter weather of 1944 to 1945 continued to be foul and this claimed the lives of many US airmen. Most US pilots been trained in relatively clear, reliable North American climates and the unforgiving English weather with its freezing fog or towering thunderclouds proved to be an enormous challenge.

Nevertheless missions had to continue in weather conditions that were often atrocious. Leaving large numbers of heavy bombers and fighters from many different airfields having to ascend through thick cloud and gather into a coherent formation for the mission to proceed. Collision was a constant fear, making skilled instrument flying and keeping to a previously agreed flight plan was essential.

For the heavy bombers, with two pilots, this was marginally less difficult, since one pilot could concentrate on the instruments while the other kept a look out. For the fighters, a new procedure had to be devised for climbing through this seemingly impenetrable soup.

Aircraft climbed in groups of four. The leader was usually the most experienced pilot and climbed using instruments, while the others flew within sight of each other. Often number four was not able to see the leader, so a tight formation was always necessary.

It was very easy to become disorientated when flying in these conditions mainly because many pilots fell victim to vertigo and did not trust their instruments. The result was often a tumble from the cloud base and no time to recover from the descent. On Saturday 13th January 1945 on a murky morning, six Mustangs were lost within the space of an hour.

2/Lt Tom Bendorf had cause to remember one such incident. It was just over a week after his crash. There were blustery snow showers with dense low-lying cloud covering most of southeastern England and the cloud base was at about 200 feet. The bombers of the 8th Air Force were marshalling for an attack on the railway infrastructure to further disrupt the flow of enemy war material and the aircraft of the 78th Fighter Group were to provide protection for the 3rd Air Division's Flying Fortresses.

Bendorf was flying as wingman for 1st Lt Herbert Elin. Elin was an experienced pilot with over 589 hours to his credit, but he had only had three hours on Mustangs and this was his first combat mission in this type of aircraft. As they climbed Bendorf could hardly see a thing in the thick cloud as he stuck close to Elin. He suddenly had a horrible sensation that they were falling not climbing. He knew that this was a common feeling and that he should ignore it and concentrate on following his leader. He also knew that once he took his eyes of the tail in front, even for a split second, he could easily be lost.

B-17F DESTROYED BY ME262
The ME262, known as the Swallow, was a fast jet fighter that was almost impossible to catch and its effects could be devastating. Fortunately for the allies, due to technical problems they were not introduced until late in the war, by which time the Luftwaffe was experiencing severe fuel shortages.

He still remained convinced that he was falling and decided to take a chance and snatch a quick glance at his instruments. He immediately saw that his worst fears were confirmed and his altimeter was unwinding at an alarming rate and that they were in a tight downward right-hand spiral. He managed to pull out in time and yell out a warning to Elin, but it was too late.

When Elin broke through the bottom of the cloud he would have been travelling at a speed of some 450 feet per second and since the cloud base was only 200 feet, he never have had a chance. He crashed near Wimpole Hall, 12 miles WNW of Duxford and the Accident Report stated simply: 'Crashed while on instruments.' The six Mustang pilots who were all ascending through cloud suffered a similar fate, and it is suspected that vertigo was the culprit in each case.

1st Lt Herbert Elin is also buried in the Cambridge American Cemetery and was one of four pilots from the 78th who were killed in flying accidents during that winter period.

By the end of January 1945 the three squadrons were getting used to their new aircraft. As their mission tally rose, so did the casualty rates. February was a particularly bad month. There were 16 strafing missions where 105 locomotives had been destroyed, plus No.19 oil tankers and many other targets, at the cost of 18 pilots. Three were taken prisoner, seven were killed and it was later discovered that the rest had managed to evade capture.

On 1st February Col Frederic Gray was posted to 8th Air Force HQ and Lt Col Olin Gilbert took his place for a short time until Col John D Landers arrived on 20th February.

Morale was low after so many recent losses and Col Landers proved to be a tonic. He was acknowledged as being one of the most brilliant and charismatic leaders of the 8th Air Force. He had previously fought in the Pacific and soon demonstrated that he was an excellent fighter pilot as well as being an excellent leader. He was to stay with Group until 1st July.

By March the situation for the Luftwaffe was getting critical. Much of the time its aircraft were grounded simply through lack of fuel. This meant that they were literally sitting ducks and as a result the 78th went from strength to strength. On 10th April 52 enemy aircraft were destroyed on the ground, with a further 43 damaged.

The long range of the Mustang meant that it could fly deep into Eastern Europe. On 16th April the Group carried out its most successful strafing mission of the War. Flying 650 miles from base, bombing attacks were made on airfields in Eastern Germany and Czechoslovakia. 135 enemy aircraft were destroyed and another 89 were damaged. This was for the loss of three pilots from the 82nd, two of whom were killed and one taken prisoner.

The final 'productive' mission came the following day when after escorting the bomber force to the Prague area the fighters swooped over airfields and destroyed 15 enemy aircraft and damaged a further 13.

The War was now all but over. There were just five further uneventful missions, the last being on 25th April when the 78th was one of two American 8th Air Force Groups to escort Avro Lancasters of 617 'Dambuster' Squadron on a raid to Hitler's Bavarian mountain home at Berchtesgarden. This ended in a bit of an anticlimax because the retreat was shrouded in snow and low cloud, so although there were some hits on the primary target, most bombs were dropped on the nearby SS barracks instead.

This brought an end to American combat flying at Duxford. The European War ended on 8th May but the war in the Far East had not finished, so training continued. It was during a training flight on 19th July 1945 that the 78th Group lost its last pilot. He was Captain James Farmer from Mississippi and this was his second accident in six weeks. His final flight ended when his aircraft crashed five miles south of Waterbeach and his grave is also in the Cambridge American Cemetery.

There followed an unsettling period as personnel were transferred out of Duxford and others replaced them, but in August, once the War was finally over, the wind-down really began. The 78th Fighter Group was gradually made ready for the return to the US and early in October it left Duxford for Camp Kilmer, New Jersey, where it was finally deactivated on 18th October.

During its 30 months at Duxford the 78th Fighter Group had completed 450 missions totalling over 89,000 flying hours. 697 enemy aircraft had been destroyed for the loss of 180 pilots. 89 of these pilots had been killed in action with a further 25 killed in accidents and 66 had became Prisoners of War.

At nearby Fowlmere the 339th Fighter Group was also on its way, with USAAF Station 378 being handed back to the RAF on 15th October. In due course, as had happened after World War I, most of this busy air base soon disappeared as the entire site reverted to farmland.

USAAF Station 357 Duxford, was formally handed back to the RAF on 1st December 1945 and as had happened after the previous conflict, while RAF Fowlmere was about to fade into oblivion, RAF Duxford was about to take on a new lease of life.

The Cold War

In December 1945, after 30 months of service with the USAAF, the RAF Standard once again flew over Duxford's main gate and a new RAF Station Commander arrived in the shape of Squadron Leader Alan Deere. Alan Deere was the first of a series of charismatic station commanders who would serve at Duxford over the next few years. He was a New Zealander, a war hero, a former Battle of Britain pilot and an experienced leader who was well liked and respected by both officers and men. He was also one of New Zealand's top scoring World War II pilots.

SPITFIRE IX
The first RAF squadron to return to Duxford after the departure of the Americans at the end of the war was 165 Squadron flying Spitfire Mark IXs. 5,665 were built and with its maximum speed of 408 mph at 25,000 feet and its service ceiling of 43,000 feet, it was a very useful machine.

Alan Christopher Deere was eight years old when he decided to become a pilot. After excelling at rugby, cricket and boxing while at school he spent two years as a law clerk. He was still under 21 when he persuaded his mother to sign his RAF entry application. He come to Britain in 1937 to join the RAF and was later posted to 54 Squadron, initially flying Gloster Gladiator biplanes, but converting to Spitfire MkIs early in 1940.

For four days in May 1940 he was credited with shooting down three Bf109s and three Bf110s. He was shot down over Dunkirk, but managed to hitch a ride on a ship and was back in London 19 hours after he had left Hornchurch. Later in the year during the Battle of Britain he destroyed seven more enemy fighters and a bomber.

By the end of the War he was credited with twenty-two confirmed victories, ten probables and eighteen damaged. His awards included a DSO, a DFC and Bar, the French Croix de Guerre and the American DFC. Last, but by no means least, he was awarded an OBE in May 1945.

No.165 Squadron was the first post-war RAF squadron to arrive at Duxford. It flew in on 18th January with its Spitfire LF (low altitude fighter) Mk IXs. In April, No.165 was joined by 91 Squadron, flying Mk 21 Spitfires. A flight of Harvards also came to be stationed at Duxford.

On 8th June 1946 a massive Victory flypast took place over London. Hundreds of aircraft were involved and both of Duxford's Spitfire squadrons took part. The Flypast was led by Group Captain Douglas Bader, who flew from North Weald with Alan Deere and Tim Vigors. Again a few weeks later on 1st August the Duxford squadrons took part in another flypast to honour US Air Force Day, this time over the US Embassy in Grosvenor Square.

The euphoria following Victory was tempered by the uncertainty of the world's political situation. Although the Soviet Union's Joseph Stalin had been an ally during the war years, he was now being seen as a threat. On 5th March 1946, Winston Churchill had sounded the alarm bells in a speech at Westminster College in the small town of Fulton, Missouri. It was here that he famously described how from Stettin in the north to Trieste on the Adriatic, an iron curtain had descended across Europe.

Duxford was about to find itself in the thick of the Cold War, but for now life went on very much as before. Immediately after the Victory Flypast, No.91 Squadron went to Lübeck in Germany for training exercises and once it returned to Duxford, No.165 Squadron, which had now been renumbered as No.66 Squadron, headed off to Lübeck in its place. In August

DEERE
New Zealander Alan Deere was eight years old when he decided to become a pilot. He was an inspired leader, he fought with distinction in the Battle of Britain and ended the war as a highly decorated Squadron Leader. He was Duxford's first post-war station commander and retired as an Air Commodore.

Wing Commander Deer moved on, to be succeeded by Wing Commander H P Burwood.

Although piston engined aircraft would continue to be used for many years to come, the new jet aircraft were becoming available in greater numbers and so squadrons began the process of conversion. No.91 Squadron took delivery of its first Meteor F3 on 30th October 1946 and No.66 Squadron also began to convert when it returned from Germany.

RAF Duxford was still using the Pressed Steel Planking (PSP) runway that had been laid by the Americans about 3½ years earlier. As well as only being barely long enough for jet aircraft, it was now showing signs of wear. Debden, had a longer concrete runway with a tarmac surface that was much more suitable and so in November No.91 Squadron moved there. Shortly after its move, No.91 Squadron was renumbered No.92 Squadron before moving back to Duxford on 15th February.

No.56 Squadron returned to Duxford in April after five years. In 1941 it had been the first squadron to try out the new Typhoons at Duxford and now was equipped with Meteors. In September a number of temporary visitors arrived ready to take part in the Battle of Britain Flypast. These included Meteors from No.74 and No.222 Squadrons, plus Tempests from No.3 and No.80 Squadrons.

By now the F3 version of the Meteor was due to be replaced by the more advanced F4, but the PSP runway at Duxford was giving trouble. On 1st February 1948, No.56 Squadron moved to Thorney Island and in March No.92 Squadron went back to Lübeck for more training. On its return to Duxford, together with No.66 Squadron, both received new Meteor F4s.

Half way through the working up period conditions at Duxford became impossible and both squadrons made a temporary move to Martlesham Heath to allow repairs to be made to the Duxford runway and for more PSP to be added to each end.

Shortly after they returned on 10th June, they were told that the Air Ministry had decided that Duxford was no longer suitable for jet aircraft. This threw the station's future into some doubt. This prompted a rethink and suggestions of laying a concrete runway alongside the existing PSP strip.

By 1949 the Cold War was truly in evidence and there was a real fear of the threat presented by the Soviet Union, which by now had built up a huge fleet of more than 700 TU-4 long-range bombers. There was talk that if an attack should come there would be only a four-minute warning, so in this event it would be imperative for our defending aircraft, the Meteors, to be able to get into the air very quickly.

This was the period of Wing Commander Herbert Moreton Pinfold's first tenure as CO at Duxford. This lasted from May 1948 to May 1951 and like Alan Deere, Pinfold was a former Battle of Britain pilot. He had joined the RAF in 1934 at the age of 21 and after a number of pre-war overseas postings, in 1940 he was an instructor at No 3 Flying Training School. On 24th August, at the height of the Battle of Britain, 27-year-old Pinfold took over as commander of No.56 Squadron at North Weald.

No.56 Squadron had suffered a number of casualties and both the previous flight commanders had been shot down before Pinfold arrived. With only eight operational pilots available the numbers were made up using Polish and Czech pilots. Pinfold believed in leading by example and during his first five days he flew 14 sorties - three of them in one day. He remained with the squadron until 29th January 1941 before returning to flying training.

During June 1949 tactical exercises took place at Duxford to gauge how the UK's defences would stand up in the event of an attack and the findings were not good. As a result it was decided that improvements to the airfield were necessary. More land was to be purchased and a new 6,000 feet concrete runway would be constructed with a new perimeter track and hard standings at various points. A new T2 hanger would be built and an operational readiness platform would be widened at each end of the runway.

While this was being done, No.66 and No.92 Squadrons moved to Linton-on-Ouse in Yorkshire. There then followed months of delay while funding was procured and work did not actually begin until 18th September 1950.

The first pilot to use the new runway was Wing Commander R N Bateson the newly appointed CO. He was another charismatic character. In 1943 he was posted as Flight Commander to No 613 Squadron, which had just re-equipped with the De Havilland Mosquito. Within three months he was appointed CO of No.613 and began to make something of a name for himself in No 2 Group, by leading low level attacks against precision targets first as a squadron commander and later as a wing leader. These raids included an attack on the Gestapo HQ in The Hague on 11 Apr 1944 and the attack on 'Shell House' in Copenhagen in March 1945.

Eleven years later on 31 July 1961, he was also to make the final 'official' take off from the same runway, when he flew a Meteor from RAF Duxford to mark it's closure as an operational RAF station.

In August 1951 two new squadrons No.64 and No.65, moved into Duxford, both flying Meteor 8s. These additions meant that by September Duxford was participating in the quick reaction alert scheme. During one exercise, 32 Meteors took off simultaneously from the parallel PSP and concrete runways and were away in a mere 75 seconds.

Bad weather always tended to have serious consequences for fighter aircraft, as shown on 29th February 1952 tragedy struck No.64 Squadron when three of its Meteor 8's were lost after bad weather suddenly closed in. One aircraft had suffered a damaged undercarriage on take-off but managed to force land at RAF Wattisham and the pilot, Flying Office F B Monge, survived.

In the second Meteor its pilot, Sergeant Verrico, got lost in eight-eighths cloud somewhere over Saffron Walden and was ordered to bail out. He also survived, but the third pilot, Flying Officer J Catchpole, became disorientated in cloud and went into a vertical dive, crashing near Debden airfield. Catchpole was killed instantly and his grave is among the war graves in Whittlesford churchyard.

Between January 1953 and December 1954, Group Captain James E Rankin took over as Station Commander at Duxford. This highly decorated airman with a distinguished war record came to Duxford following a period as Air Attaché in Dublin.

Jamie Rankin, as he was known, had joined the RAF in 1935 but after his initial training flew for some time with the Fleet Air Arm on HMS Glorious. After a period as an instructor with No 5 OTU he was attached to 64 Squadron for a short while before taking command of 92 Squadron in February 1941 flying Spitfire Mk Vs. By June he had been awarded a DFC for 9 victories and three months later he became Wing Leader at Biggin Hill, receiving his first DSO in November. The following summer he received a Bar to his DSO closely followed, in the early autumn of 1942 by a Bar to his DFC.

He was credited with destroying 17 enemy aircraft and a V-1 flying bomb.

It was during Jamie Rankin's period that on the rainy evening of 2nd June 1953, Wing Commander Jimmy Wallace DSO, DFC, Officer Commander Flying, led the Duxford Wing in a Coronation Day flypast at 12,000 feet over Buckingham Palace. The formation was made up of seven wings comprising 144 Meteor 8s and 24 Sabres. This wing on 15th May 1954 escorted the Queen on her return in the Royal Yacht Britannia from her post-coronation world tour of the Dominions and Colonies. Jimmy Wallace later became Deputy Captain of The Queen's Flight

That summer the station received a Spitfire LF 16 to be used for flypasts and general ceremonial purposes. In December Jamie Rankin was succeeded as CO by Group Captain DF MacDonald, whose tenure lasted until Herbert Pinfold returned to Duxford for a second tour as Station Commander in April 1956. By now Pinfold had been promoted to Group Captain having spent three years as Air Attaché in Rome.

Unfortunately on 24th January 1956 the ceremonial Spitfire was written off in an accident. It was patched up and was put on static display and was later replaced by a similar aircraft.

During that year it had been decided that Duxford would become an all-weather station. 64 Squadron was the first to switch to Meteor NF12 night fighters and shortly after updated NF14s were added. Early the following year No.65 Squadron took over the daylight role and began to receive Hawker Hunters in place of its Meteors. No.65 Squadron flew its last operational Meteor sortie on 21st March.

The 1957 the Battle of Britain Day display was held on 14th September, and two features were outstanding. The first was an early outing by the English Electric P1. This was the prototype of the Lightning and came to Duxford straight from the Farnborough Air Show,

The other major feature was a farewell Spitfire demonstration by Jeffrey Quill who was about to retire from test flying. In 1933 Jeffrey Quill had been a member of the Meteorological Flight at Duxford but when he was offered a job working as a test pilot for the Supermarine Company had decided that this was a more promising opportunity than staying in the RAF. Supermarine was then best known as a builder of sports aircraft, but would become famous for building the Spitfire. It was Jeffrey Quill who delivered the first Mk I Spitfire to Duxford's No.19 Squadron in August 1938.

Gloster Javelin FAW7s replaced No.64 Squadron's Meteor night fighters in September 1958. The Javelin was the world's first twin-engine delta-wing fighter. It had been designed to operate at high altitudes and in all weathers, day or night. It was introduced into RAF service with 46 Squadron at RAF

HAWKER HUNTER

The Hawker Hunter was one of the sleekest post war fighters to be stationed at Duxford with 56 Squadron. In 1959 the CO, Sq Ldr Maughan, won the competition celebrating the 50th anniversary of the first crossing of the English Channel by Louis Blériot by travelling from Paris to London in 40 minutes 44 seconds. He used a Hawker Hunter for part of his journey.

Odium in 1956, destined to become the RAF's main night fighter. Eventually it was in use by 14 squadrons, with the last being withdrawn from service in 1968.

In August 1958, Herbert Morton Pinfold's three-year tour as CO of RAF Duxford came to an end before his retirement from the Service in October.

Group Captain Edgar Norman Ryder was Pinfold's successor. He too had had a distinguished and eventful career. He was born in India and became a Maths teacher at a school in Worcester. However, one night during a drinking session with the Classics master they got talking about the prospect of war and after one thing led to another, Ryder joined the RAF.

In 1937 he became a member of No.41 Squadron, stationed at RAF Catterick in North Yorkshire. On 3rd April 1940, still with No.41 Squadron, he was said to have been flying the first Spitfire to be shot down in an engagement with the Luftwaffe. After being dispatched to look for a lone Heinkel He111 that had reportedly been attacking fishing boats off Whitby, Ryder soon found the trawlers that had been "sorely knocked about" by the enemy bomber.

It seemed that the trawlers had put up quite a fight because they had managed to disable one of the Heinkel's engines. The German plane was limping along about 200 feet above the sea and Ryder gave it a four-second burst. At the same time one of the trawlers let fly with a Lewis gun and Ryder saw the aircraft pancake onto the sea and the five-man crew scramble out.

As Ryder was firing at the German aircraft he felt a couple of bumps against his own aircraft but thought nothing of it until smoke and fumes began to fill his cockpit. He was only about 50 feet above the sea and he knew that he would never make the 15 miles back to Hartlepool, so instead he decided to land on the water.

Unfortunately the sea was a lot rougher than he had originally thought and the Spitfire promptly sank. Yet somehow he managed to get to the surface and as he was struggling to stay afloat, the trawler found him and he was hauled aboard. The trawler proceeded to pick up the crew of the Heinkel. It took the trawler six hours to reach Hartlepool, during which time Ryder was terribly seasick. His exploits that afternoon earned him a DFC.

In May the squadron flew down to Hornchurch to provide air cover for the Dunkirk evacuation and later in the year they were back at Hornchurch again for the Battle of Britain. 49 pilots from number No.41 were involved in the Battle and the squadron scored 100 kills, but there was still a 44%

casualty rate. Ryder was shot down for the second time on 27th September during a day of intense air combat, but this time bailed out safely.

He then took over command of No.56 Squadron at North Weald until it moved to Duxford in June 1941. Ryder did not stay with the squadron because he was promoted to Wing Commander and became CO of the Kenley Wing, but not for long. Shortly after his appointment, on 31st October 1941, he was shot down for a third time while he was flying a Spitfire Mk VB of No.485 (NZ) Squadron.

This time he crashed on the wrong side and came down on the beach near Dunkirk where he was captured. He became a prisoner at Stalag Luft 3 at Sagan in Silesia, where he proved to be a very troublesome POW. He was involved in nine attempted tunnel escapes, plus a further three schemes, one of which involved smuggling himself out of the camp in the back of a Luftwaffe lorry and trying to steal an aircraft.

In addition to the DFC that he was awarded in 1940, he received a Bar to that in July 1941 and a Mention in Despatches for his escape work when a POW. Following his retirement he was awarded a CBE.

In 1909 the London *Daily Mail* had awarded £1,000 to Louis Blériot for being the first person to cross the English Channel in a heavier than air craft. To commemorate the 50th anniversary The *Mail* decided to hold a competition in the summer of 1959 for the fastest time to get from the Arc de Triomphe in Paris to Marble Arch in London, or *vice versa*. Wing Commander Norman Ryder was captain of the RAF team.

The first prize of £5,000 was won by Squadron Leader Maughan, CO of Duxford's No.65 Squadron, with a time of 40 minutes 44 seconds. Not far off was Wing Commander Ryder who came in third with a time of 42 minutes 6 seconds and his prize was £1,500. Both airmen achieved their times by a combination of running, riding a motor cycle, flying in a helicopter and flying in a No.65 Squadron Hawker Hunter. Ryder later said that his greatest memory of the day was an 85-mph ride through Paris on the back of a motorcycle.

Apart from these little interludes of excitement, much of Duxford's activity involved regular, highly secret and often tedious activity associated with the Cold War. Lighter moments did come when the squadrons were called upon to take part in ceremonial flypasts. On 20th February 1960 Wing Commander Storey, CO of the Duxford Wing, led 36 of No.65 Squadron's Hunters over Buckingham Palace to celebrate the birth of Prince Andrew. A similar formation was led up the Mall on 11th June to celebrate the Queen's Official Birthday.

On 6th July 1960, exactly 25 years after the 1935 Jubilee review, No.64 and No.65 Squadrons both celebrated 25 years of service. During the ceremony Marshal of the Royal Air Force Sir William Dickinson, who had taken part in the 1935 review, presented new standards to both squadrons.

Shortly after this, No.64 Squadron's Javelins were replaced by later Mk 9s, with re-heat, but the days of Duxford as an operational station were already numbered. The next generation of jets would need a longer runway. Not only that, but the station's already aging buildings, that 20 years earlier the USAAF had found so comfortable during wartime, were now in serious need of refurbishment or replacement.

In addition Britain's defence requirements were changing and its fighter umbrella was moving northwards. After careful consideration, it was decided that RAF Duxford no longer had a future and that it should close. Wing Commander Ryder departed in September 1960. His successor, Group Captain A L Winskill was appointed for the final months until the station ceased to be operational in the summer of the following year.

Archie Winskill was yet another of the characters of the RAF. Shortly after joining No.41 Squadron, on 14 August 1941, he was part of an escort for a formation of Blenheims attacking a target in Lille when they were set upon by a group of Bf109s. Winskill was able to destroy one before being shot down. Baling out, he landed close to a French farmer, who hid him until he was handed over to the 'Pat' escape line. Winskill became the first pilot to return to England using the route through Spain and Gibraltar.

However, this experience led to him being banned from leading any of his units over France so after a while he was made commander of No 232 Squadron and given the task of taking it to North Africa. On 18 January 1943, he was once again shot down, this time into the sea but he was able to swim ashore. Unfortunately he was behind enemy lines, but managed to get back to the Allied lines on foot. This made him one of the few to have been shot down and evaded capture twice.

His final total for the war was four confirmed enemy destroyed and two shared, one probable, one damaged, two destroyed on the ground and one damaged on the ground.

After Duxford he went on to become Director of RAF Public Relations and during this time he had to prepare a press release on the crash of a

GLOSTER JAVELIN

Gloster Javelins came to Duxford in September 1958 to replace 64 Squadron's Meteor jets. Eventually they went on to become the RAF's main night fighter during this stage of the Cold War and were in use by 14 squadrons. They were finally withdrawn from service in 1968.

Whirlwind helicopter of The Queen's Flight, in which the Captain of the Flight was killed. Shortly afterwards, he was appointed to the post himself, and one he held from 1968 to 1980 making him the second longest serving Captain of the Queen's Flight. He was knighted at a private audience on 20 Feb 1980.

It was a sad time for RAF Duxford and preparations for its closure had already begun when Archie Winskill arrived. No.65 Squadron was first to go, being disbanded on 31st March 1961 closely followed by the Station Flight, being disbanded in May.

On 28th July No.64 Squadron moved to Waterbeach and that was about it. Three days later Air Vice Marshal R N Bateson, a former CO of Duxford returned in his personal Meteor NF 14 and in a final symbolic flight brought to an end 44 years of operational life at RAF Duxford.

Epilogue: The Station that
Refused to Die

I n 1961, after 44 unbroken years of military service, of which the last 37 had been as a fighter station, the RAF finally departed from Duxford. Within a short time grass had begun to grow along the perimeter tracks and the whole place soon began to take on an air of general neglect. There was talk about using it for a prison and even discussion about placing Britain's Blue Streak ICBMs here, but that came to nothing when the project was cancelled.

The Ministry of Defence still owned the site, but it was clear that it had no real use for it. There was scant security and local people even used the runway for racing their cars and teaching teenagers to drive. In 1967 the Ministry was approached with a proposition to use the former RAF station for location sequences of the film *Battle of Britain*. Agreement was reached and in the spring of 1968 the film unit moved in.

Somewhere around £38,000 was spent on sprucing up the parts of the base that would appear in the film. Since it was impossible to use archive footage, it was necessary to film all the flight sequences. The prodcuers soon encountered the problems of finding a sufficient number of aircraft. Eventually 27 Spitfires were rounded up that could be used for active filming, plus a number of others that could be used for static shots. At this point, there were only six Hurricanes left in the world and one of these had been bought as a job lot off a scrap heap by a Canadian pilot who then rebuilt it and flew it across the Atlantic in order to appear in the film.

Fortunately the Heinkel He111s and Messerschmitt Bf109s were not a problem since they were still being used by the Spanish Air Force. About 50 Heinkels were loaned to the production company, who then bought 20 de-commissioned Bf109s. Most of the aerial filming took place over Cambridgeshire and over the North Sea using a B-25 Mitchell as a camera platform. By opening the bomb-bay doors the camera could be lowered and shoot over a 360 degree field and be operated by the cameraman sitting immediately above.

During the filming, as part of a simulated air raid, Duxford's single bay Belfast hanger was blown up. The film cost twelve million dollars to make. It was a big budget production, packed with stars and this helps explain why it made a loss on its first release.

One positive effect of the film was that it provoked interest in Duxford and led to the formation of the East Anglian Aviation Society. The Society started the fight to save Duxford airfield. Somehow the Society managed to keep going and it even attracted some rare aircraft, but in spite of a considerable amount of enthusiasm and devotion it was clear that the whole project was financially doomed.

DUXFORD MUSEUM

Duxford continues to be operational for private aircraft, but it is now also the home to some of the important elements of the Imperial War Museum including Air Space, telling the story of British and Commonwealth aviation, the American Air Museum in Britain and the exhibition of Land Warfare. Regular displays of vintage aircraft take place throughout the summer.

The saviour came in the shape of the Imperial War Museum. The IWM wanted a site where it could store, restore and possibly display some of its larger exhibits, particularly its aircraft. So in 1971 an agreement was reached to allow it to use part of the airfield to house historic aircraft. The first to be flown in was a Sea Vixen that arrived in March 1972. Other aircraft subsequently arrived and in October 1973 the aerodrome was opened for a special air day.

The upshot of all this was that the Imperial War Museum was given full use of the aerodrome as an outstation for its collection. Sadly there were differences of opinion between the Imperial War Museum and the East Anglian Aviation Society, which resulted in the EAAS moving its collection out of Duxford and into an alternative museum in the former control tower of RAF Bassingbourn. This had been an active station between 1938 and 1969 and was a USAAF 8th Air Force bomber base from 1942 to 1945. The Society was renamed the Tower Museum.

Some members of the East Anglian Aviation Society decided to remain and they formed the nucleus of the Duxford Aviation Society. In June 1975 the Duxford Aviation Society and the Imperial War Museum jointly organised a two-day display. This included aerobatics and appearances by a Fairy Swordfish and a Sea Fury.

By June 1976 the War Museum's collection had grown to the point where it was decided to open on a daily basis. This proved to be a great success and numbers of visitors continued to rise.

A problem that arose that year was the projected building of the new M11 that would link London with Cambridge and the main cross-country route from the East Coast ports to the Midlands. The proposed new motorway would cut across the end of Duxford's runway and shorten it by 1,500 feet. Fortunately a compromise was reached and although the runway was shortened, its length remains a respectable 4,931 feet.

Over the years many aircraft have continued to arrive at Duxford, either for display or restoration. One of the early arrivals on 20th August 1977 was the first pre-production Concord 01 G-AXDN. As the collection continued to grow a priority was the need for more display space and there have been a number of different projects.

The first major project was a new 'super hanger' to house and display larger aircraft such as the Lancaster and the Sunderland Flying Boat. This was opened in 1985 by HRH Prince Andrew, Duke of York.

The Imperial War Museum was also anxious to display some of its collection of historic military vehicles in realistic settings and in September 1992 a new Land Warfare Hall was opened at the far end of the airfield.

Many saw the need for somewhere to commemorate the achievements and sacrifice of the United States Air Force during World War II and the 30,000 American airmen who lost their lives serving in British bases. In August 1997 the Queen officially opened the new purpose-built American air museum.

Five years later in September 2002, George Bush Senior, No.41st President of the United States and the Prince of Wales rededicated the building following further major improvements. After 15 years the 1985 super hanger was no longer big enough to appropriately display some of the larger aircraft in the collection, so a new project was initiated to raise funding for the construction of a new AirSpace building. This was completed in 2007.

Even now flying continues at Duxford and during the summer months there are regular displays of vintage and veteran aircraft that attract thousands of visitors. Thousands more people from all over the world also visit the museum to see its static displays. There is a thriving and well-established educational programme and there are workshops for the restoration and maintenance of the historic aircraft.

Although RAF Duxford is no longer a military airfield, it continues to be a living airfield. To the thousands who visit each year it serves as a lasting reminder of the many hundreds of European, Commonwealth and North American men and women who over the years have heroically served there and in many cases given up their lives for the sake of freedom.

BIBLIOGRAPHY

Action Stations Vol 1 Eastern England : Michael Bowyer : Crécy Publishing

Air Battle for Dunkirk : Norman Franks : Grub Street Publishing

An Illustrated History of the RAF : Roy Conyers Nesbit : Colour Library Books

Battles of World War II – Vol 20 Dieppe : Osprey Publishing

Cambridgeshire Airfields in the Second World War : Graham Smith : Countryside Books

Combat Aircraft : Bill Gunston : Salamander Books

Duxford Diary 1942-1945 : The Duxford Aviation Society

East Anglia 1939 : R Douglas Brown : Terence Dalton

East Anglia 1940 : R Douglas Brown : Terence Dalton

Essex Airfields in the Second World War : Graham Smith : Countryside Books

Fighter : Len Deighton : Triad Panther

Fighter – Technology – Facts - History : Ralf Leinburger : Parragon

Fighter Boys : Patrick Bishop : Harper Perennial

Flying Colours – Epic Story of Douglas Bader : Laddie Lucas : Hutchinson

Ghost Fields of Norfolk : Roderick McKenzie : Larks Press

Hertfordshire Airfields in the Second World War : Graham Smith : Countryside Books

Life's Too Short To Cry : Tim Vigors : Bounty Books

Lincolnshire Airfields in the Second World War : Graham Smith : Countryside Books

Military Airfields of East Anglia Norfolk & Suffolk : Ken Delve ; Crowood

Norfolk Airfields in the Second World War : Graham Smith : Countryside Books

RAF Duxford : Richard C Smith : Grub Street Publishing

Spitfire Pilot : David Crook : Bounty Books

Spitfire Squadron : Dilip Sarkar : Air Research Publications (Including "Spitfire" by Sq/Ldr Brian Lane)

Spitfire - The Biography : Jonathan Glancy : Atlantic Books

St Clement Danes : Pitkin Guide

Suffolk Airfields in the Second World War : Graham Smith : Countryside Books

The Bader Wing : John Frayn Turner : Pen & Sword Aviation

The Battle of Britain : James Alexander : Trans Atlantic Press

The Battle of Britain : Jon Lake : Silverdale Books

The Battle of Britain : Patrick Bishop : Quereus

The Mighty Eighth in the Second World War : Graham Smith : Countryside Books

The Narrow Margin : Derek Wood with Derek Dempster : Tri Service Press

USAAF Fighter Stories : Ian McLachlan : Sutton Publishing

Winged Victory : Johnnie Johnson and Laddie Lucas : Limited Editions

Other books in this series

Heroes of the RAF No.1
– No.43 Squadron
Heroes of the RAF No.2
– Guy Gibson
Heroes of the RAF No.3
– No.50 Squadron

No.19 Squadron **4, 9, 13, 15, 16, 17, 18, 19, 20, 22, 24, 25, 27, 28, 30, 31, 33, 34, 36, 39, 40, 41, 43, 44, 45, 46, 47, 48, 49, 53, 55, 56, 59, 60, 63, 67, 71, 72, 73, 74, 75, 76, 118**

No.41 Squadron **17, 22, 76, 119, 121**

No.66 Squadron **18, 20, 23, 27, 41, 113, 114, 115, 116**

No.92 Squadron **27, 114, 115, 116**

No.222 Squadron **23, 26, 27, 29, 30, 33, 34, 114**

No.229 Squadron **41**

No.264 Squadron **27, 30, 33**

No.266 Squadron **58, 59, 74, 79**

No.310 Squadron **36, 39, 41, 42, 44, 52, 53, 55, 59, 60, 63, 66, 67, 73, 74, 75**

No.611 Squadron **20, 23, 42, 44, 45, 47, 50, 53, 56, 58, 59, 60, 63, 66,**

Arnold, Gen. Hap **94, 96**

Avro 504 **11, 14**

Avro Tutor **14, 15**

B-17 Flying Fortress **81, 89, 97, 101, 102, 103,**

Bader, Gp Cptp Douglas, **5, 22, 24, 25, 26, 27, 29, 30, 33, 34, 39, 43, 44, 50, 52, 53, 56, 57, 60, 62, 65, 69, 72, 73, 76, 84, 113**

Blenheim, Bristol **20, 23, 26, 78, 81, 121,**

Broadhurst, Harry "Broady" **16, 17, 83, 84**

Bulldog, Bristol **13, 15, 17**

Churchill, Winston **27, 65, 88, 113**

Coltishall, RAF **33, 39, 40, 41, 42, 44, 47, 50, 53, 56, 58, 66, 74, 86**

Coward, Noel **80, 81**

Crosby, Bing **91, 93**

Deere, Air Commodore Alan **112, 113, 114, 115,**

Defiant, Boulton Paul **27, 30, 35**

DH9A **11, 12**

Dieppe Raid **77, 81, 83, 84**

Dornier Do215 **44, 53, 60**

Dowding, Air Chief Marshal Sir Hugh **18, 46, 51, 56, 64, 69, 70, 81**

Focke Wulf FW190 **49, 77, 82, 83, 84, 85, 91, 92, 93, 96, 98, 100, 107**

Fowlmere, RAF **9, 10, 31, 33, 41, 43, 44, 45, 46, 49, 50, 53, 56, 59, 63, 66, 71, 74, 75, 76, 80, 97, 98, 111**

Gauntlet, Gloster **16, 17, 18, 19**

Heinkel He111 **23, 31, 46, 77, 119, 123**

Hitler, Adolf **32, 36, 37, 38, 47, 60, 64, 111**

Hope, Bob **91, 92, 95**

Hunter, Hawker **117, 118, 120**

Hurricane, Hawker **18, 22, 23, 30, 33, 34, 36, 41, 42, 43, 44, 48,50, 52, 55, 56, 59, 60, 62, 63, 67, 73, 74, 75, 76, 77, 79, 81, 123**

Javelin **118, 120, 121, 122**

Johnson Air Vice Marshal, James "Johnnie" **46, 47, 48, 56, 66, 82**

Lane, Fl Lt Brian **28, 29, 30, 31, 32, 44, 49, 50, 59, 60, 73, 75, 76,**

Leigh-Mallory, Air Vice Marshal Trafford **5, 38, 39, 40, 43, 48, 56, 58, 67, 68, 69, 70, 81, 83, 84**

Luftwaffe **27, 28, 31, 32, 36, 38, 39, 40, 42, 46, 47, 51, 53, 56, 59, 60, 61, 62, 64, 65, 66, 81, 82, 84, 90, 94, 97, 104, 110, 119, 120**

Messerschmitt Bf109 **29, 34, 44, 47, 52, 53, 60, 61, 62, 63, 64, 66, 67, 73, 77, 83, 91, 93, 94, 98, 100, 113, 121, 123**

Messerschmitt Bf110 **29, 40, 41, 43, 44, 53, 55, 73, 77, 113**

Meteorological Flight **13, 48, 118**

Mosquito, De Havilland **5, 71, 78, 79, 116**

Mustang, North American P-51 **79, 81, 86, 97, 106, 107, 108, 109, 110**

P-47 Thunderbolt **79, 86, 89, 90, 91, 98**

Park, Air Vice Marshal Keith **4, 5, 14, 42, 56, 68, 69, 70**

Pinkham Sqn Ldr Philip **28, 30, 39, 43, 44, 45, 47, 48, 49**

Royal Flying Corps (RFC) **7, 8, 9**

Siskin, Armstrong-Whitworth **12, 13, 15**

Smuts, Lt-Gen Jan **7, 8**

Spitfire, Supermarine **4, 18, 19, 20, 21, 222, 23, 24, 25, 26, 27, 28, 31, 32, 33, 34, 36, 37, 39, 40, 41, 43, 44, 45, 47, 49, 50, 53, 55, 56, 59, 60, 62, 63, 64, 66, 67, 71, 73, 74, 75, 79, 82, 83, 84, 97, 112, 113, 119, 120, 123**

Trenchard, Maj-Gen Hugh **8, 10, 11**

Typhoon, Hawker **5, 72, 75, 77, 79, 80, 81, 83, 84, 85, 114**

USAAF **5, 79, 80, 85, 87, 88, 91, 92, 94, 96, 97, 111, 112, 121**

Vigors, P.O. Tim **26, 27, 30, 34, 113**

Whittle, Sir Frank **14**